Seeds of Bitterness

Dr. Charlotte Russell Johnson

Author of

A Journey to Hell & Back

A production of
Reaching Beyond, Inc.
www.charlotterjohnson.com
P. O. Box 12364
Columbus, GA 31917-2364
(706) 573-5942
Also available @ www.charlotterjohnson.com

Bitter

Lyrical Payne

I'm angry, I'm bitter
I'm tired; I'm hurt.
I'm done pretending,
It just won't work.

I remember what you did
I remember what you said
I know I should move on,
But, I just wish you were dead.

You hurt me; you scarred me
Then you walked away free.
You took my power from me
And you won't let me be.

I don't see you, we don't speak,
But, you're still haunting me
I'm bitter and I'm mad
My anger is controlling me

You don't remember what you did
Or maybe you just don't care,
But, I'm stuck with this anger
And it just isn't fair
Why do you get to be happy
Why do you get to move on
Why am I stuck with the memories
Why does it seem like you won

I can never forgive you
I can never be free
You took my happiness
You stole my power from me

I try to let go
I try to move past
I try to forget
But, I know it won't last

I'm bitter, I'm angry,
I'm hurt and I'm tired
You've forgotten I exist,
But, I still feel this fire

They're thoughts in my head
You'll never know they're there
It's not like anything will change
It's not like you care

Wait, this is crazy
I know I have problems
How can I let go
What can I do to solve them
I know I need help
I have to get this out of me
I have to let go of this bitterness
I need to be free
I need to forgive
I need to snatch my power back
I need help to get through this
I need to get this demon off my back

I have to pray for help
I have to seek and find God
I have to take back my life
I have to look up above

Bitterness isn't healthy
Bitterness only hurts me
Bitterness keeps me bound,
But, I must become free

I've been holding this too long
I have to get this out of me
Lord, please help
Lord, I need you to be free

I feel such relief
I feel so free
I let go of my bitterness
You no longer control me

I'm letting you go
Right this minute, this hour
I'm bitter no more
I'm reclaiming my power

In Memory

Of

Wiley Owens

"Uncle Wiley"

July 3, 1916 - March 13, 1985

Dedicated

To

Carolyn Delores Alexander

"Aunt Pickle"

March 2, 1942-February 24, 2014

"Gone but not Forgotten"

INSIDE THE SEEDS

Margarette Johnson Davis

September 2, 1949 - July 22, 2016

Preface

My first book, *A Journey to Hell and Back* was an autobiographical account of my life. It details major events in my life, which almost destroyed me. These events were shared to provide hope and encouragement to others.

My second book, *Daddy's Hugs* exhorts the role of fathers in the lives of children. The book praises and provides examples of fathers who take a diligent role in parenting. It shares my appreciation for several men in my life who were positive male role models.

My third book, *A Journey to Hell and Back: The Flip Side* tells two sides of the journey. *The Flip Side* is my husband, Buck's version of our lives. We shared our separate struggles, which became a common struggle. The book focused on different past experiences that influenced our future.

In *Grace Under Fire*, I discussed unfavorable or controversial issues to the body of Christ. My husband has been portrayed accurately, although sometimes unflatteringly. The purpose of the book wasn't flattery. Actually, it discussed the dangers of a flattering woman.

Mama May I, my fifth book, explores the extensive effects of substance abuse and its effects on the family system. *Mama's Pearls*, my sixth book, relates words of wisdom that my mother has shared with me. It is a tribute to the woman who prayed me out of hell. It is also humorous.

My seventh book, *Breaking the Curse,* explores family dysfunctions and secrets. It challenges each of us to face hidden demons in our families. We are encouraged to take a stand for the littlest victims.

Kissin' Hell Goodbye, the eighth book, uses the poetry in songs to convey the entire drama. This is a very pithy way of providing the reader with knowledge about the character's feelings while invoking an emotional response from them based on their own past experiences with the songs.

My ninth book, *Oil for the Wounded* explores the difference between a wound and a hurt. It then provides the answer for overcoming these wounds. God gave me the answer, "You have to pour oil into the wound." That was the birth of *Oil for the Wounded.*

Now comes the question, "What happens when wounds aren't healed? What happens when you don't know how deeply you have been hurt? What happens when you reject the oil that God has provided? Thus we have *Seeds of Bitterness.*

All scripture references are from the King James Bible unless otherwise noted.

Introduction by Earline Hall

Seeds of Bitterness is the tenth book in Dr. Charlotte Johnson's series of motivational text. Dr. Johnson is able to use the metaphor of a seed of bitterness to explain how forgiveness and resentment can grow if not resolved. Revenge, retribution, our misguided attempts to ensure others are accountable for their actions, emotional blackmail, and other psychological tools or weapons to restore balance with those who have wronged us, can serve as fertilizer for our seeds of bitterness.

The novel is Dr. Johnson's exploration into the reason and causes for her current circumstances. Ralph Ellison's *Invisible Man* and President Barack Obama's memoir, *Dreams from My Father* offered similar narratives of self-exploration. The story is told from (the narrator's) Dr. Johnson's present as she delves into her past. Thus, the narrator has hindsight in how her story is told, as she is already aware of the outcome.

Dr. Johnson is able to master

traditional literary techniques to provide her readers with clear and concise descriptions of factual events while providing the passion and excitement of modern television dramas such as ABC's Revenge based on Alexandre Dumas's novel, *The Count of Monte Cristo*. I found myself riveted by Dr. Johnson's struggle to identify her actions and true motivations and how this impacts her sense of self and others. She enlists the aid of her trusted friends and family members in her narrative; the impact on their lives is documented. She contemplates how she will proceed forward after making startling revelations about herself and others.

The book offers guidance on acceptance, forgiveness, and growth. After *Oil for the Wounded*, Dr. Johnson took a three-year hiatus from writing and returns with a fresh and vibrant infusion to her prose. This novel delves further into self-exploration of the cause of emotional stress and traumas and their impact on our growth but offers an even grittier and stark approach that leads the reader to self-examine their own pain and role in retaining and deifying it. Several major characters are written out of the series in this book. This leads to Dr. Johnson's exegesis.

This book is an excellent self-help book for those suffering from unresolved anger and bitterness but also entertains and inspires all readers to be the best possible version of themselves. They say that revenge is a dish best served cold, but no one prior to Dr. Johnson has pointed out so poignantly how it chills the body and the soul with bitterness. Dr. Johnson offers hope for the hopeless, and joy in the midst of sorrow, for those willing to face themselves in the mirror and to do the work needed.

Bitterness! Bitterness!!

And went to him, and bound up his wounds, pouring in oil and wine, and set him on his own beast, and brought him to an inn, and took care of him.

Luke 10:34

One day, as I was doing a book signing, a man whom I consider a long-time friend walked up to me. I was always glad to see him. He is also a minister. Over the years, we have shared many spirited and thought-provoking conversations. This time was different. He had been ill for some time. Perhaps, it was the medication; I cannot say. Whatever the reason, he began to rant and rave about something. I have no idea what he was talking about or what set him off. As he continued the tirade, I watched in shocked silence.

"But I say to you that every one who is angry with his brother shall be guilty before the court;

and whoever shall say to his brother 'Raca,' shall be guilty before the supreme court; and whoever shall say, 'You fool,' shall be guilty enough to go into the hell of fire."

Matthew 5:22

The public interaction was totally inappropriate. It was disrespectful to both the location and purpose of the venue. If the store manager had been inclined, there would have been an arrest for disorderly conduct. This would have been even more scandalous.

I am disgusted with my life. Let me complain freely. I will speak in the bitterness of my soul.
Job 10:1 NLT

After my continued refusal to engage in conversation or argue with him, he begins to pound his fist on each of the books on my table. As he did this, he was also screaming, "Bitterness! Bitterness! Spreading bitterness!"

My mother was sitting at the table with me. She has known this minister longer than I have. Neither of us had ever observed him responding to any situation with any hint of anger, rage, or bitterness. He had always seemed to be a very humble man. My mother who is normally quick to respond to any situation, (even quicker when she believes her children are being attacked) was left speechless. The look of shock and disbelief on her face voiced the words that she was unable to speak.

Good sense makes one slow to anger, and it is his glory to overlook an offense.
Proverbs 19:11

The manager of the store was standing nearby watching the interaction. He is normally very aloof. However, after the minister walked off, he walked over to us. He was concerned about our welfare. We explained that we had known the minister for approximately thirty years. We further explained that we had never seen him spreading bitterness. During those thirty years, we had never seen him so hostile and volatile. We had never seen him "Spreading bitterness! Bitterness!!"

The Merriam-Webster Dictionary defines bitterness as:

- having a strong and often unpleasant flavor that is the opposite of sweet
- causing painful emotions

- felt or experienced in a strong and unpleasant way
- angry and unhappy because of unfair treatment

My purpose in writing this book is not to change or challenge that definition. My intention is to explore the topic to expand our growth. The word bitterness can be used in a variety of ways and serve various functions within a sentence.

The Merriam-Webster Dictionary defines a seed as:

- a small object produced by a plant from which a new plant can grow
- the beginning of something which continues to develop or grow

By definition, a seed of bitterness is the beginning of something which continues to develop or grow, causing painful emotions that are felt or experienced in a strong and unpleasant way. This seed can cause a person to be angry and unhappy because of perceived unfair treatment.

A man of wrath stirs up strife, and one given to anger causes much transgression.
Proverbs 29:22

Resentment and bitterness occur early in the Bible. Cain was angry that God accepted Abel's sacrifice and not his sacrifice. Instead of examining his actions and dealing with those negative feelings by admitting his own part in the situation and considering God's will, he buried his anger under feelings of resentment which grew until he killed his brother.

In *Oil for the Wounded,* I discussed many examples of things that cause hurts and wounds. The answer to overcoming these wounds was also discussed in depth. Wounds, hurts, jealousy, discouragements, and disappointments, whether caused intentionally or unintentionally can become the seeds of bitterness.

Faithful are the wounds of a friend; but the kisses of an enemy are deceitful.
Proverbs 27:6

The wounds may be caused by friendly or enemy fire. Indeed, sometimes wounds occur accidentally. The wounds that occur because of friendly fire are precipitated by someone who is considered a friend or companion in arms. It is extremely difficult to accept these types of wounds. They are unexpected and they can cause deep and deadly wounds. Because they are unexpected, the wounds are often deep and hard to heal. They can cause doubt, undue speculation, resentment, and animosity between friends, church members, coworkers, family members, or comrades.

A hurt is usually temporary. Hurts that go untreated can become wounds. If a wound goes untreated for an extended period of time, it develops a deep root. The seed has been planted deeply. The deeper the seed is planted the deeper the root will be. The deeper the root, the harder it is to heal the wound. It takes a wise and skillful counselor to facilitate the healing of the wound. It takes a wise person to pour oil into the wound.

A wise man feareth, and departeth from evil: but
the fool rageth, and is confident.
He that is soon angry dealeth foolishly:
and a man of wicked devices is hated.
Proverbs 14:16, 17

There are times when people will refuse healing. Pride can hinder a person from admitting they have been wounded. They prefer to pretend that they are too strong to be hurt. Pretending that they are not emotionally vulnerable to hurt hinders them from honestly dealing with the pain. Others may attempt to justify or rationalize the wound. Any delay in the wound being healed allows time for the seeds of bitterness to grow.

Wounds are usually accompanied by outward manifestations. Anger, resentment, jealousy, insecurity, paranoia, and a wide range of emotions are often triggered by wounds. These are outward manifestations of the seeds that have begun to grow. Substance abuse, violence, promiscuity, and criminal activities are often the offspring of wounds.

Bitter Victory

A Victim's Honest Feelings

Lyrical Payne

With all the jacked up, foul things you've done to me...
You used me till you were through with me.
You left me sore, battered, and you bruised me.
You made me feel like that was all I was meant to be.
How could you have done that to me?
I thought we were a family.
I'm hurt mentally, physically, emotionally.
I feel as if I'm dying and not just spiritually.
What more could this evil world do to me?
Can everyone tell that I'm in pain, and bleeding freely?
If they can, then why won't someone reach out to me?
I'm walking alone in the dark; can someone please shine a light for me?
I've forgotten the sounds of happiness, joy, love,

and peace.
Can someone please just call out to me?
I'm stumbling around in this world blind.
Can someone please just help me to see?
With all the ugliness in the world, can someone
help me find just a little bit of beauty?
With that entire monster did to me,
Why wasn't someone there for me?
I'm struggling to get away, why won't someone
help me?
Even though I've matured, is it still so hard to
see the little kid in me?
Is it because you're all blind, do you only see
what you want to see?
Y'all say that I'm evil, y'all talk about me
Y'all hate me and say that I live sardonically
I know it's no excuse, but maybe he did this to
me
I'm screaming for help, why won't anyone hear
me?
Can't you feel the little girl in me, tugging at your
knee?

You people tell me it's easy to find victory,
But maybe it's not for everyone; maybe it's not out there for me
I cried out for help, where's my victory?
I came forth with the truth, and still, I haven't received 
I went to the law; they were no help to me
Tell me who's gonna help me get my victory?
Why are y'all protecting him? He's the bad guy can't you see?
Why does he deserve to take my victory?
This just isn't fair, what about me?

Barbara Owens Morgan Eberhart

November 24, 1938 - April 18, 2002

Inside Out

The Lord said to Moses and Aaron, "If anyone has a swelling or a rash or discolored skin that might develop into a serious skin disease, that person must be brought to Aaron the priest or to one of his sons. The priest will examine the affected area of the skin. If the hair in the affected area has turned white and the problem appears to be more than skin-deep, it is a serious skin disease, and the priest who examines it must pronounce the person ceremonially unclean.

Leviticus 13:13 NLT

Leprosy has been thought to be a disease of the skin. It is best classified, however, as a disease of the nervous system. The leprosy bacterium attacks the nerves. It is spread by multiple skin contacts. It is also spread by droplets from the upper respiratory tracts. These nasal secretions are transmitted from person to person.

Biblical leprosy is a powerful symbol reminding us of how bitterness spreads and its horrible consequences. Like leprosy, the seeds of bitterness start out small, but will continue to spread if it goes undiagnosed and is left untreated. Bitterness leads to other sins and causes great damage to our relationship with God and others.

See to it that no one falls short of the grace of God and that no bitter root grows up to cause trouble and defile many.
Hebrews 12:15 (NIV)

The Bible compares bitterness to a "root" and

asserts that many have been "defiled" by it. The scriptures speak of a "root of bitterness" because it often goes deep and hidden beneath the surface. The potential effect upon our life can be widespread and hard to uproot. Our thoughts and actions can be deeply embedded in roots of bitterness.

My daughter remembers vividly a funeral that she attended. After the committal service, a woman that she knew was holding on to the casket. She was crying profusely and refused to be comforted. The woman repeatedly cried, "I'm sorry Mama! I'm sorry Mama!"

It was a noble gesture, but it was too late to make amends with her mother. The event changed Earline's life. She became more appreciative of the family that God has given her. She constantly tells her family how much she loves them.

When bitterness is allowed to take root, it becomes an increasingly deadly and destructive motivating force. If left unchecked, it will completely pollute our lives and eventually destroy our relationship with God. Unresolved bitterness will severely damage our relationships with our closest loved ones and friends.

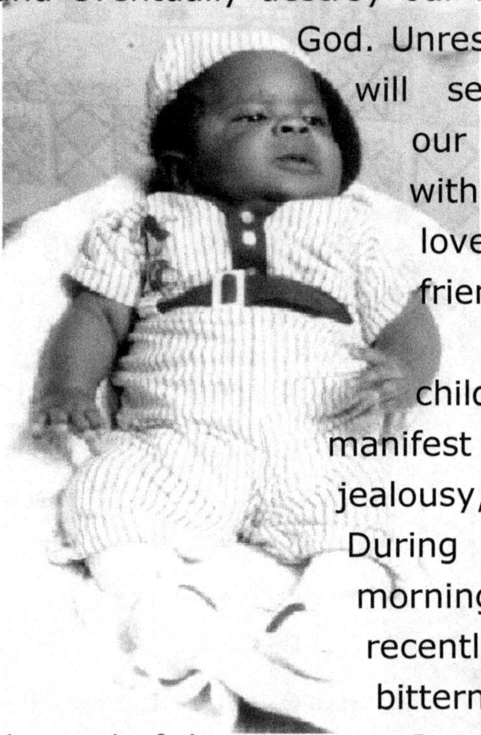

Even young children can manifest signs of anger, jealousy, and bitterness. During my Sunday morning message recently, I spoke about bitterness. Towards the end of the message, I stressed that when you remain bitter towards someone, you give that person control over your life. I asked this question, "Who do you want to have control over your life?" One of our youth who is nine-years-old responded, "God!"

It made me proud to see that she is building her biblical knowledge. I replied, "You have God in you!" My granddaughter who turned two-years-old a couple of months ago blurted out, "I've got God in me!"

This was actually a phrase that I borrowed from a story my son shared with me. Herman has a lot of godchildren. This young lady is approximately five-years-old. While being harassed by a bully at school, she decided not to respond with anger or bitterness. Instead, she responded with wisdom beyond her years.

She looked straight at the person seeking to antagonize her. With full confidence, she said, "I ain't afraid of you! I've got God in me and you have the devil in you!" What a wonderful response. She rejected the seeds of bitterness.

But know this, that in the last days perilous times will come: For men will be lovers of

themselves, lovers of money, boasters,
proud, blasphemers, disobedient to parents,
unthankful, unholy, unloving, unforgiving,
slanderers, without self-control, brutal,
despisers of good, traitors, headstrong, haughty,
lovers of pleasure rather than lovers of
God, having a form of godliness
but denying its power.
And from such people turn away!
2 Timothy 3:3-5

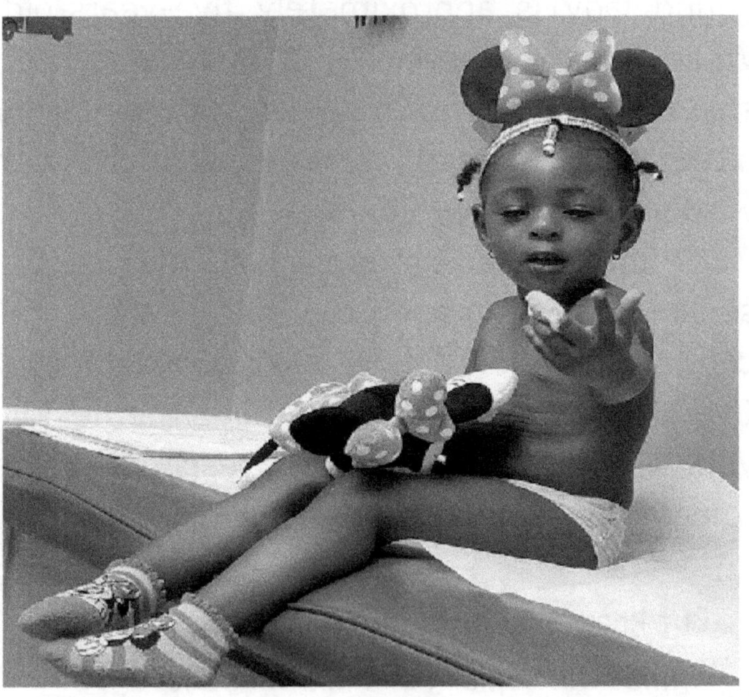

We are living in perilous times and sometimes, even Christians do not respond correctly to the things that happen in our lives. There is a natural progression that ultimately leads to the seeds of bitterness. It usually begins in this order: HURT, ANGER, and BITTERNESS. HURT must be dealt with scripturally or it will lead to ANGER. Anger must be dealt with scripturally or it will lead to BITTERNESS.

Hurt that is resolved based on the Word of God will never become anger. Any deviation from the Word will result in anger. Unresolved anger will lead to the next step, bitterness. Bitterness begins on the inside of us, but it does not end there.

When bitterness spreads to the outside, it will affect everyone who comes into contact with the person. It was mandated in biblical times that the people with leprosy cry out, "Unclean! Unclean!" So it is with the seeds of bitterness. Bitterness cries out, "Unclean! Unclean!"

I do love u!

Shelena

As time presses on and things start to change,
I have changed too, thanks to you.
I have done things to you.
You may never forget the hurt and the pain that I
have caused you and the sadness in your eyes,
all due to my ugly ways and lies.
How is it that you do not despise me, but continue
to care, loving me beyond the compare?
How I look at these things.
Suddenly a bell starts to ring inside my head
letting me know I have been a fool.
So all I ask of you is to forgive me please and
never let me go because I do love you.

Planting

But we have renounced disgraceful, underhanded ways. We refuse to practice cunning or to tamper with God's word, but by the open statement of the truth we would commend ourselves to everyone's conscience in the sight of God.

2 Corinthians 4:2

When *Kissin' Hell Goodbye* ended, my fairy tale ending appeared to be lost. This is obviously not the way that I envisioned the ending of this chapter of my life. In many ways, it appeared that I failed. It certainly felt like a failure. After devoting countless years to the rehabilitation of my husband, he walked away in a very painful and humiliating way. In my eyes, I had wasted most of my life waiting for him to accept Christ as his personal savior and become the man I knew God had called him to be. Throughout our relationship, I saw drugs as the enemy. There was a false assumption that once the drugs were no longer an issue, we would have the perfect relationship.

There were several problems with my plan. I had never heard of ***crack denial.*** I was focused on the outward manifestation of a deeper problem. There were seeds that had been sown in both of our lives. Because substance abuse and prison had been major factors in our lives, we hadn't learned to live together with clean hearts.

then the Lord knows how to rescue the godly from trials, and to keep the unrighteous under punishment until the day of judgment, and especially those who indulge in the lust of defiling passion and despise authority. Bold and willful, they do not tremble as they blaspheme the glorious ones, whereas angels, though greater in might and power, do not pronounce a blasphemous judgment against them before the Lord.

2 Peter 2:9-11

An addict uses drugs as a solution to

their problems. Not dealing with problems often causes more problems. To completely end drug addiction a person has to feel more competent and develop better coping skills for living without drug usage. Part of this process involves discovering hidden seeds of bitterness, jealousy, shame, malice, and deceit;

Conquering an addiction requires more than abstaining from the addictive behavior or activity. This involves examining and changing all the associated feelings and behaviors attached to the addiction. The denial associated with the drugs often hinders this from happening. The formidable task of altering the addict's behavior and ultimately helping them in overcoming their addiction is made doubly hard because, in order for this to happen, the behavior of the codependent also needs to change.

When I changed my behavior towards Buck, it changed our relationship. For years, I had treated him as if he was one of my children. He had become accustomed to being pampered. As I sacrificed for my children, I also sacrificed for Buck. In doing this, my own needs often went unmet. When my needs went ignored, it had the potential for becoming the source of the seeds of bitterness.

But if ye have bitter envying and strife in your hearts, glory not, and lie not against the truth.

James 3:14

When I decided this would have to change, Buck didn't like it. While I firmly stood my ground, he resisted making these changes. His rebellion turned to hurt and pain. This was another opportunity for the seeds of bitterness to grow. I couldn't see his pain. I saw selfishness, ingratitude, etc. It wasn't that I had turned against him. However, I had come to realize that to become the head of the household; he needed to take responsibility for his actions and behavior.

But we have renounced disgraceful, underhanded ways. We refuse to practice cunning or to tamper with God's word, but by the open statement of the truth we would commend ourselves to everyone's conscience in the sight of God.
2 Corinthians 4:2 ESV

Crack denial made it impossible for us to have a healthy marriage or relationship. Buck had his own ideas. He saw nothing wrong with himself or his behavior. Not only was he defensive, he was convinced that I had contributed to the problems that he was having. It was difficult for him to relate to a Charlotte, who wasn't catering to his every need. I was trying to teach him a different lesson. In order for him to assume the role as head of the household, he would also need to take responsibility for the household.

Sometimes, he took the offensive. This was to draw attention away from himself. After a few weeks, it was obvious there was something seriously wrong. I questioned Buck, but he denied that anything had happened during his last incarceration.

Although I was familiar with many short-term effects of drug usage and many of the obvious long-term effects of drug usage, I was confused by what was happening. I didn't know about the lingering effects of crack. Some of the outward physical effects were obvious, rapid aging, dental decay, and accelerated graying. My knowledge of heroin was more thorough, but that demon had already been overcome.

Then she lulled him to sleep on her knees, and called for a man and had him shave off the seven locks of his head. Then she began to torment him, and his strength left him.

Judges 16:19 NKJV

Somehow, I had been lulled into a false sense of security. This may have been my own form of denial to cope with his drug usage. I needed to believe that once he stopped using drugs, we would have a normal life. My major concern had been with his overdosing. Sure, I had seen the commercials, read the books, and watched the films. It never became reality.

My frustration had grown for months. Outside forces were also causing interference in our marriage. I was tired of the years of struggle. It would have been easy for me to take the initiative to resolve our conflicts. The conflicts were actually minor. Instead of resolving our conflicts, I stilled my heart towards him. This was easy. Each time I spoke to him, he was defensive. There was an edge in his voice. The seeds of bitterness were starting to grow in both of our hearts.

"The man who hates and divorces his wife," says the LORD, the God of Israel, "does violence to the one he should protect," says the LORD Almighty. So be on your guard,
and do not be unfaithful.
Malachi 2:16

Soon we were headed for our third divorce. Before it was filed or finalized, Buck became involved with his first wife. Things became ugly and murky. The drama was supposed to be over. At least, that was what I thought. Rather than focusing on Buck or his response, I began searching for answers. As the days went by, God began to deliver me from resentment, anger, revenge, and unforgiveness. He was delivering me from the seeds of bitterness. These were emotions that I was familiar with. They were also emotions that I thought I had overcome. Surely, I had forgiven Buck for his infidelities. He continuously apologized for those relationships. I didn't doubt his sincerity. The last relationship had served to break a stronghold in his life. Before that relationship, he had roving eyes. He no longer has this problem.

Approximately a year later, the divorce was finalized. Following each of our divorces, the separation allowed us to reexamine the importance of our marriage and the importance of our relationship. Each time we divorced, the marriage was dissolved legally, but not emotionally. The attachment between us was always clear when we were separated. This time, outside manipulators had clouded the picture.

Let no one split apart
what God has joined together."
Mark 10:9 NLT

Signing the papers should have brought a measure of relief for him. It didn't! I understood the feeling.

Divorce never severs what God has joined together. Now that we had signed the papers, Buck wanted to talk to me. We talked for a while, standing outside of his car. Buck and I shared our common feelings.

We needed to make a trip to the credit union. He had given me a check as partial settlement of the divorce. We needed to arrange for the additional monthly payments to come directly from his account to my account. **Dangerous**! Whenever possible, make a clean break. This process was not going to go smoothly and would require that we have additional contact.

Wisdom is the principal thing;
therefore get wisdom:
and with all thy getting get understanding.
Proverbs 4:7

He had an issue that he wanted to get straight. If he hadn't been so serious, it would have been funny. There was something that he had been holding against me. It was a dead man! Charlie had been dead for some time when we had this conversation. As we stood outside the credit union, he looked sternly at me and said, "You really embarrassed me! You went out with Charlie! He always said that he would get you back! You made it look as if it were true!"

It hardly deserved an answer, but I tried. It was another seed of bitterness. The incident with Charlie happened after our first divorce. Buck and I hadn't seen each other in several months. When Charlie was released from prison, he called me. He knew that Buck was locked up. He probably knew that we were divorced – not that it would have made any difference. It had been years since we had seen each other. He had really been studying the Bible in prison and had given his life to Christ. This was something that Charlie wanted to share with me. I wanted to encourage him.

Immediately, Buck remarried his first

wife. They had been divorced for more than twenty years. During that time, they had minimal contact. Many things had changed in those years. The seeds of mistrust, doubt, and bitterness had been sown.

A [self-confident] fool's lips bring contention,
and his mouth invites a beating.
Proverbs 18:6 AB

We both knew he was making a mistake. Pride often hinders him from admitting mistakes until complete damage has been done. After a few months, we rekindled our relationship. Shortly after Buck and I started seeing each other again, he shared a new concern with me. This time, his concern wasn't about me. It was about someone else and with a new twist. Now, I wasn't surprised by what he said. It just surprised me that he admitted this concern to me.

Let all bitterness, and wrath, and anger,
and clamour, and evil speaking,

be put away from you, with all malice:
Ephesians 4:31

On numerous occasions, Buck seriously said to me, "I know what's going on! I need to be able to prove it. If you would just get it on tape, I could set it up. I'm telling you, I almost caught it one time. They were coming out of the back room at the gym. They tried to play it off. I know about women like that! I'm just not comfortable with her friends. Even at church, there are certain kind of people that she likes to sit by. If you would do this for me, you would be surprised at how fast everything would fall into place. You would have everything that you want!"

If he had proof, this would give him grounds for the divorce. Considering the way things had happened, I didn't think that he needed an excuse to file for the divorce. Although I'm not sure who it was, he needed proof to satisfy somebody. After hearing this for months, I suggested that he get someone else to tape it for him. I suggested a particular relative should be asked to make the tape. Afterward, Buck stopped asking me about it.

At the same time that Buck was trying to verify **his suspicions**, he openly did just what he wanted to do. Actually, I don't know if his suspicions were based on reality or paranoia based on her admitted past experiences. There were things in her past that he was unable to forget. Buck often talked about her past experiences. Her recent release from prison may have exacerbated his concern.

During the separation, I did not feel free or comfortable getting involved in another relationship. I continued to pray for Buck's health, safety, and happiness. More than anything else I prayed for his salvation. As time passed, I was convinced he was doing well.

O give thanks unto the LORD, for [he is] good: for his mercy [endureth] for ever.
Psalms 107:1

One Saturday, I was thanking God for

Buck's deliverance from drugs and prison. Many of our friends had died because of the direct or indirect effects of drugs. In the process of praising God, I acknowledged that perhaps Buck needed to be separated from me to enhance his dependence on God. Later that afternoon, I received a call notifying me that Buck had been rushed to the hospital. He was experiencing problems with his heart. I was approximately three blocks from the hospital that he had been taken to. My mother and my granddaughter, LaToya, were with me. We began to pray.

LaToya was extremely upset and threatened to walk to the hospital. This would have caused him additional stress. He would have been glad to see her, but other people would not have felt the same. Although he had a strong relationship with her, he had almost completely cut off contact with her when we separated. The seeds of bitterness were already growing and this was added to the plant.

By arranging to get regular updates on his status, I was able to appease LaToya temporarily. The next day, we were able to talk to him.

But if the unbelieving depart, let him depart. A brother or a sister is not under bondage in such cases: but God hath called us to peace.
1 Corinthians 7:15

In the months prior to his attack, he had been under a lot of stress. They were obviously unhappy, but he was determined that he would not be the one to end the marriage. He continued to stay in touch with us. He was sure things would end soon. He asked me to be patient. He was sure that we would have an opportunity to correct our mistakes.

"I have said these things to you, that in me you may have peace. In the world you will have tribulation. But take heart;
I have overcome the world."
John 16:33

Buck's feelings about the marriage were mutual. She was also unhappy. One day, she announced her intention to move out. This was expected and he was prepared for the things that ensued. Nevertheless, the seeds of bitterness were sown.

It was seven years before that relationship ended. It ended as painfully as it began. A lot can happen in seven years. Buck's health declined. She went to prison for several months. Trust was destroyed. Secrets were kept. Insecurities were abounding. Insults left deep wounds. The devastation was apparent. Self-esteem was shattered. The relationship left a lot of baggage. The seeds of bitterness were sown and they grew to maturity.

It seemed to be our destiny to try our relationship again. It appeared that the separation had forced both of us to grow and mature. For years, I had wanted Buck to have a closer walk with the Lord. Additionally, I wanted him to have a spiritual mentor. From our conversations, it appeared the separation had provided an opportunity for all of this to take place.

Ironically, a year before this happened, a close friend of ours dreamed a dream. In the dream, Buck was going through some difficult times in his relationship. In the dream, the woman who he was involved with was packing and secretly removing property from the apartment. One day, while Buck was at work a U-Haul truck backed into the driveway of the apartment. The truck stopped very close to the front door. She said that she thought it was going to hit the apartment. She saw two men exit the truck. The truck was quickly packed. When Buck arrived home, almost everything was gone.

Buck was eventually warned about the dream. Within days, he noticed things were disappearing. He was excited that his freedom was getting close. One morning, he decided that he needed to move the things that he valued from the apartment. When he returned from work that evening, the apartment was almost completely empty.

The neighbors told Buck about how quickly the apartment had been emptied.

They said that they thought the U-Haul was going to back into the apartment. They said there were three men. When he heard this summary of the day's events from the neighbors, Buck began to laugh.

Be ye not unequally yoked together with
unbelievers: for what fellowship hath
righteousness with unrighteousness? and what
communion hath light with darkness?
2 Corinthians 6:14

When two people share the same level of commitment to the Lord, it should strengthen any marriage. When God has united two individuals into one, the bond should be unbreakable. The bond between us was still strong. It seemed that all of the turmoil during our relationship had made our relationship stronger.

We made a lot of promises to our friends and families. We promised that there would never be another divorce. We intend to keep this promise. Has this been easy? NO! There is an old song that says, "Starting all over again is going to rough on us, but I pray to the Lord to help us make it." During those years of separation, the seeds of bitterness were sown.

Come now, and let us reason together, saith the LORD: though your sins be as scarlet, they shall be as white as snow; though they be red like crimson, they shall be as wool.

Isaiah 1:18

For our fourth wedding, we knew that we needed the blood of Jesus Christ to cover a lot of wounds, a lot of hurts, and seeds of bitterness. The colors for the wedding were chosen appropriately, cream and crimson.

God didn't fail! In the end, He did what I asked. I prayed fervently for Him to rescue the rescuer. Throughout my life, I have been attempting to rescue people who didn't want to be rescued. This was often done at great sacrifice. I sacrificed myself.

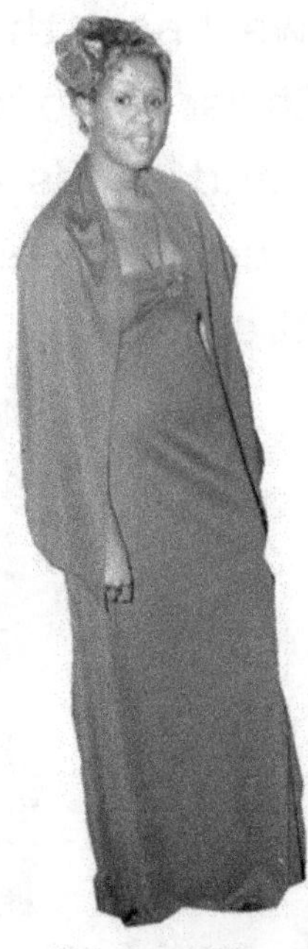

But now you have been united with Christ Jesus. Once you were far away from God, but now you have been brought near to Hm through the blood of Christ.

From Our Hearts

God through His amazing love and grace has given us another miracle. We are grateful that His unfailing love has graced our love. Because God joined our hearts and spirits together as one, we have been unable to destroy what He created. Our love is a testimony of God's awesome power and authority. We willingly yield to His authority. We sanctify ourselves for His purpose and His glory. We solicit your prayers as we endeavor to walk worthy of the bonds of holy matrimony. To God be the glory for what He has done in our lives.

Thanks

We would like to express thanks to our family, and friends for all their love and support. Thank you all for sharing this special day with us.

Tilling the Ground

Then the Lord said to Cain, 'Why are you angry? And why has your countenance fallen? If you do well, will not your countenance be lifted up? And if you do not do well, sin is crouching at the door; and its desire is for you, but you must master it

Genesis 4:6-7 NAS

Tilling the ground or soil means to prepare (soil, a piece of land, etc.) for growing crops. There is a deep wound in all of our lives. Circumstances often prepare our hearts to receive the seeds of bitterness. They can become a very destructive force in our life. Although we think the wound has healed, there are times that it appears to reopen for no apparent reason. When we rehearse or meditate on previous injustice, hurt, pain, wounds, and disappointments, it may renew the pain or reveal the seeds of bitterness that were previously unknown.

"Do you still hold fast your integrity?

Curse God and die."

Job 2:9

In the Bible Job's wife allows herself to become bitter. Anger would be an understandable reaction to all that God was allowing to happen to her family. In one day, her children die and her family's assets are completely destroyed. Instead of accepting God's sovereignty and following Job's example, or even being honest and talking with God, she allowed anger to turn to resentment which leads her into bitterness. The seeds of bitterness take root. Her frustration and bitterness led her to encourage her husband, Job, to curse God.

When Job's three friends, Eliphaz the Temanite, Bildad the Shuhite and Zophar the Naamathite, heard about all the troubles that had come upon him, they set out from their homes and met together by agreement to go and sympathize with him and comfort him.

Job 2:11 NIV

Aggravating Job's situation are his friends. Although their intentions are good, they cause Job to rehearse and meditate on his troubles and problems. They meant to encourage him. They wanted to help Job find a solution to his problems. However, their efforts serve to keep the pain alive and fresh. When we meditate on our problems, it illuminates them. The problems are magnified and begin to grow astronomically. Each time we tell the story, it sounds worse.

When people share their pain, they often expect sympathy or empathy. If they find this lacking, they may begin to add additional details. This may be intentional or unintentional. As Job begins to defend himself from his well-meaning friends, self-righteousness begins to set in. he begins to boast of his righteousness.

She said to them, "Do not call me Naomi;
Call me Mara, for the Almighty has dealt very bitterly with me.
Ruth 1:20

Recently, someone who loves me dearly attempted to encourage me. As they reminded me of all the things that I have to be thankful for, it also reminded me of the numerous mistakes that I have made in my

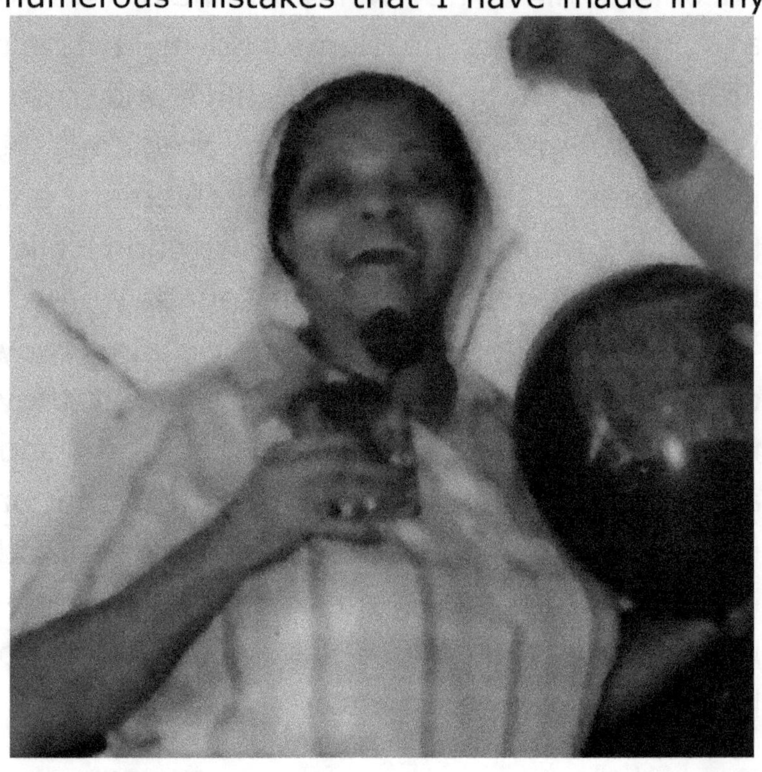

life. Mistakes that can't be undone often lead to feelings of regret and negative assessment. As I began to enumerate my numerous failures, depression began to creep in. While in this state, I began to focus on how much of my life has been wasted.

This well-meaning person continued their attempts to encourage me by telling me how much good I have done with my life. They began to tell me of the numerous people who have found hope through my testimony. This served to remind of failed relationships, bad relationships, bad choices, hurt, pain, mistreatment, disappointments, disasters, heartache, and wounds. In the end, I felt a seed of bitterness beginning to grow. Bitterness is easy to fall into, but it is also possible to reject bitterness and return to faith in God.

"Let all bitterness and wrath and anger and
clamor and slander be put away from you,
along with all malice."
Ephesians 4:31 ESV

Bitterness and resentment often come from a belief that someone is being unfair or not giving us what we believe we deserve. This attitude often comes from flawed thinking. Those who expect the most often give the least. While they feel entitled to receive, they feel no compulsion to give. The Bible tells us to reject bitterness.

For the kingdom of heaven of heaven is like a landowner who went out early in the morning to hire workers for his vineyard. And after agreeing with the workers for the standard wage, he sent them into his vineyard. When it was about nine o'clock in the morning, he went out again and saw others standing around in the market place without work. And he said to them, "You go into the vineyard too and I will give you whatever is right." So they went. When he went out again about noon and three o'clock that afternoon, he did the same thing.
Matthew 20:1-5

One day, a child asked me for money to purchase an item from the store. After I gave her the funds, she went inside the store to purchase the item. At the same time, my mother who was accompanying me went into the store to purchase an item for her companion. When the child returned from the store and saw her companion opening what she had been given, she was obviously upset.

Let your character or moral disposition be free from love of money [including greed, avarice, lust, and craving for earthly possessions] and be satisfied with your present [circumstances and with what you have]; for He [God] Himself has said, I will not in any way fail you nor give you up nor leave you without support. [I will] not, [I will] not, [I will] not in any degree leave you helpless nor forsake nor let [you] down (relax My hold on you)! [Assuredly not!]

Hebrews 13:5 AB

With her voice raised, she said, "Where did you get that from? I didn't get any!"

Both purchases were equivalent in price. I explained to her, she had received what she asked for. Now she felt slighted because she didn't receive what the other person received.

The first part of chapter 20 of Matthew's gospel records a very similar story that Jesus told. It is about the wages paid to the workers in the vineyard. The master agreed to pay each worker a certain amount and he kept his word. The twist here is that many of those who began working in the vineyard earlier in the day believed that they deserved more than the agreed upon wage.

See to it that no one fails to obtain the grace of God; that no 'root of bitterness' springs up and causes trouble, and by it many become defiled.
Hebrews 12:15 ESV

Anger is often a natural sometimes physiological response. If anger goes unchecked it can do substantial damage. It can blind us to our part in the situation. It can hinder all ability to have empathy and compassion for others. Even when our anger is just, we must not allow it control our actions or beliefs. The Bible warns us to take every thought captive and to submit to God. This will drive us to forgive others and keep our anger from turning to resentment and bitterness.

Be wise, my son, and bring joy to my heart;
then I can answer anyone
who treats me with contempt.
Proverbs 27:11 NIV

Everyone faces many trials; however, these trials are not in vain. God uses them to do a work in us. His goal is to develop us into mature Christians. He has a purpose and a plan for our life. When we become bitter during our trials, it delays our spiritual growth.

Consider it pure joy, my brothers, whenever you face trials of many kinds, because you know that the testing of your faith develops perseverance. Perseverance must finish its work so that you may be mature and complete,
not lacking anything.
James 1:2-4

God uses the tough times in our lives to purify and refine us. The tough times help to make us mature and complete Christians. Furthermore, God will not permit us to remain in the same precarious situations all of our lives. There will be a time and a season for everything. Seasons will change. In God's appointed time, He will deliver us.

The righteous cry out, and the LORD hears

them; he delivers them from all their troubles.

Psalm 34:17

When we attempt to run from our trials, we delay our spiritual development. The testing of our faith develops us into a mature and complete Christian.

God is willing to heal resentment and bitterness if we will allow Him. He can heal our hearts and cause us to forgive others. It begins with putting our trust in Him. If we don't let Him, we will reap the consequences of our actions or failure to act. Cain, like many people today, wanted to come to God, but he wanted to do it his way. He believed in God, and he wanted God's approval, but he wanted to come to God on his terms, not on God's terms. Resentment and bitterness are often aimed toward God. This can lead to slander against Him. It is the epitome of taking His name in vain.

And no man putteth new wine into old bottles:
else the new wine doth burst the bottles,
and the wine is spilled,
and the bottles will be marred:
but new wine must be put into new bottles.
Mark 2:22

Set on Edge

"Why do you quote this proverb concerning the land of Israel: 'The parents have eaten sour grapes, but their children's mouths pucker at the taste'? Ezekiel 18:2 NLT

When we are insulted, our natural inclination is to return an insult for an insult. When we hurt our natural instinct is to hurt back. You find out what you really believe when others mistreat you. Sometimes the real test of your faith is what you don't do or say. Sometimes you'll be a better Christian by not saying or doing anything at all.

Let the word of Christ richly dwell within you, with all wisdom teaching and admonishing one another with psalms and hymns and spiritual songs, singing with thankfulness in your hearts to God.
Colossians 3:16 NAS

Most of us are familiar with the detrimental effects of child abuse and neglect. Examples of physical abuse include overt harmful behaviors such as: hitting, biting, shaking, choking, kicking, burning, and throwing objects.

Then there's emotional abuse which might include behaviors such as verbal assaults, screaming, excessive criticism, cursing, intimidating, rejecting, or blaming. It may include humor that is sarcastic or detrimental to the child's self-image. It can take the form of teasing, taunting, belittling, or ridiculing, name calling, ignoring or treating the child with indifference, and deliberately setting up a competitive situation in which the child is sure to lose. Overpowering a child, so that they feel helpless or captive, such as tickling until breathless; and constant family conflicts are also a form of abuse. But what happens to a child that has gone thru this type of abuse? Sadly, many of them will repeat this negative behavior.

"How long, you simpletons, will you insist on being simpleminded? How long will you mockers relish

your mocking? How long will
you fools hate knowledge?
Proverbs 1:22 NIV

Family traits are often passed down from parents to children, and this cycle has been repeated for thousands of years. Some of these traits may be positive. However, the negative and destructive behaviors are also passed down within families. These negative behaviors are often rooted deeply to the seeds of bitterness. Scarcely a child hasn't found fault with parental behavior. Children pledge that they will not repeat the mistakes of their parents. However, in many families, the behavior is repeated.

Simeon and Levi are brothers; their swords are
implements of violence. Let my soul not enter
into their council; let not my glory be united with
their assembly; because in their anger they slew
men, and in their self-will they lamed
oxen. Cursed be their anger, for it is fierce; and
their wrath, for it is cruel.
I will disperse them in Jacob,

and scatter them in Israel.

Genesis 49:5-7 NASB

My mother shared with me a story of a man who was fired. He came home and beat his wife. The wife, in turn, beat the children. With no one else to blame, the children killed the cat. Those who have been hurt often hurt others. Sadly, the person that they deem a safe target to vent their anger upon is often an innocent bystander.

Travis Morrison

"Trav"

MY OTHER SON

November 2, 1985- May 10, 2015

Thirsty

One who is full loathes honey from the comb,
but to the hungry even what is bitter
tastes sweet.
Proverbs 27:7 NIV

We all have necessary desires and needs that God has ordained and purposed. We have desires to be significant, to be loved, to feel needed, to feel wanted, to feel important, to give love, to feel secure, to have a purpose, and we want our lives to have meaning and promise. God wants us to have these things. In an ideal world, these needs are met in our family of origin. However, we know that God is the ultimate source of our provision.

Without natural affection, trucebreakers,
false accusers, incontinent, fierce,
despisers of those that are good,
2 Timothy 3:3

Sadly, we live in a time when the need for natural affection goes unmet in the family of origin. It is even sadder when those needs go unmet within the church family. The love of many has waxed cold. Those who grow up with unmet needs often have seeds of bitterness. What happens when those needs go unmet? Does the need cease to exist? How do you mend these broken hearts?

People will be lovers of themselves, lovers of money, boastful, proud, abusive, disobedient to their parents, ungrateful, unholy, without love, unforgiving, slanderous, without self-control, brutal, not lovers of the good,
2 Timothy 3:2-3

We live in a fallen world. Our failures are often an attempt to obtain the essential things that we have missed in life. We may attempt to obtain good things in the wrong way. Sometimes when we fail, we're covered with shame and guilt. These feelings can become consuming. The seeds of bitterness will begin to manifest. It can become easier to blame someone else for our failures. Sometimes when we fail we become depressed.

In the thirst to have their needs met people may form cliques and begin criticizing and excluding others. This causes deep division within families, churches, social organizations, professional organizations, and civic/social organizations. That's a bad thing.

Some will seek fulfillment through We seek connection and intimacy through illicit sex, pornography, and emotional affairs. These relationships are contrary to the word of God. They will destroy any organization. This includes marriages and ruin families.

"Blessed *are* they which do hunger and thirst after righteousness: for they shall be filled."
Matthew 5:6

The thirst is real, but real satisfaction can only be found in a meaningful relationship with God. He placed a place of longing within us that only He can fill. When we hunger and thirst after righteousness, God has promised to fill the need.

Jesus answered and said to her, "Everyone who drinks of this water shall thirst again; but whoever drinks of the water that I shall give him shall never thirst; but the water that I shall give him shall become in him a well of water springing up to eternal life."
John 4:13-14

There are some things that quench our thirst better than others. Water has traditionally been the recommended beverage. Now, some prefer Gatorade or Powerade. Yet these beverages can never quench the thirst for some things. No matter how much you drink, some thirsts will remain. There also disorders that occur from drinking too much. No water is more satisfying or sustaining than the water Jesus provides.

For I will pour water upon him that is thirsty,

and floods upon the dry ground: I will pour my spirit upon thy seed, and my blessing upon thine offspring:
Isaiah 44:3

The seed referred to in the previous verse is our offsprings, our descendants, and our children. However, the principle is the same. Nothing Jesus touches remains the same. If we give Him our seeds of bitterness, He will give us beauty for our ashes. He will give us joy in the midst sadness. We can exchange our garments of sadness, our garments of anger, our garments of jealousy, our garments of heaviness, our garments of spitefulness, our garments of defeat, our garments of revenge, our garments of hatred, our garments of manipulation, and our garments of bitterness, for the garment of praise.

Ho, every one that thirsteth, come ye to the waters, and he that hath no money; come ye, buy, and eat; yea, come, buy wine and milk without money and without price.

Wherefore do ye spend money for *that which is* not bread? and your labour for that which satisfieth not? hearken diligently unto me, and eat ye that which is good, and let your soul delight itself in fatness.

Isaiah 55: 1-2

In an effort to quench their thirst, many turn to artificial forms of gratification. Isaiah 55 begins with an invitation that highlights man's needs. It puts emphasis on the futility of life without God. It stresses the inability of the things men traditionally put their trust in to provide lasting meaning. Wealth, fame, social status, professional organizations, possessions, praise, and pleasure fail to provide meaningful or lasting satisfaction. Those who strive for these artificial fillers become easy prey for predators who will exploit them. Things like wealth, position, and power will never bring long-term satisfaction.

Serve the LORD with reverent fear, and rejoice with trembling. Submit to God's royal son, or He will become angry, and you will be destroyed in the midst of all your activities--for His anger flares up in an instant. But what joy for all who take refuge in Him!
Psalm 2:11-12, NLT

Because people fear the loss of what is purported to bring happiness, they often strive against God. Some desperately cling to that which cannot fulfill, i.e., positions, false relationships, false pride, outward beauty, titles, and material possessions. These are often traps that prevent us from finding and developing meaningful relationships with God.

I remember the
days of old; I
meditate on all
Thy doings; I
muse on the
work of Thy
hands. I stretch
out my hands to
Thee; My soul
longs for Thee, as
a parched land. [Selah].
Psalm 143:5-6

God alone can quench our thirst. Mankind was created for God and at the center of our being is a void that only God can fill. He is a jealous God. He wants our fondest thoughts. He wants to be the desire of our hearts. He wants to fill that void within each of us. He wants to quench our thirst.

Repeat

"Be angry, and yet do not sin; do not let the sun go down on your anger"
Ephesians 2:26 NASB

Beware of anger and bitterness and of the people who are controlled by them. If you aren't careful, you will learn their evil ways. The more we lean on the words of men, the farther we get away from scripture and dependence on God. Many leaders have been able to lead people down wrong paths. These paths will ultimately cause harm. Ungodly leaders are able to take otherwise normal, intelligent human beings and convince them that anger and bitterness are acceptable emotions. Although they may feel these emotions are wrong when they are the recipient or the victim of an angry and bitter tirade, the victim will often repeat the behavior.

According to many Christians, a leader has special privileges and is exalted above the members of their congregation and anyone else. Many leaders accept and encourage this exaltation. This is extremely **dangerous**! When we lift anyone up in God's place, we set them up for failure. It also places us in a position to be deeply wounded.

"But be not ye called Rabbi: for one is your Master, even Christ; and all you are brethren. And call no man your father upon the earth, for one is your Father, who is in heaven"
Matthew 23:8-9

God is still a jealous God. He wants our fondest desires and thoughts to be of Him. The greater we exalt anyone, the deeper the wound will be that severs this ungodly attachment.

During our days of innocence or ignorance, we often make many foolish declarations. This is a familiar one, "When I grow up, I'll never treat my children like that." This one is all too familiar, "When I get married, I'm going to..." What about ministers? "When I become a pastor, I will never treat my members the way I was treated in ministry."

Many times as we are observing negative treatment that is rooted in bitterness, it is becoming the foundation for the future. The justification for treating people in this manner may become essential truths. This makes it easy to manipulate people into doing things they might not otherwise do.

Do not be misled: "Bad company corrupts good character. Come back to your senses as you ought, and stop sinning; for there are some who are ignorant of God--I say this to your shame."
1 Corinthians 15:33-34 NIV

Sometimes, the wounds are so deep that the victim will seek to justify the behavior. It can be difficult to accept that someone you care deeply for is mistreating you. Rather than dealing with the seed of bitterness that begins to grow, they will rationalize it. Even sadder, the victim will often repeat the pattern and mistreat others.

The wrath of God is being revealed from heaven against all the godlessness and wickedness of men who suppress the truth by their wickedness.
Romans 1:18

Is it possible that they have forgotten how it felt when they were treated in the same deplorable manner? Have they become blind to the truth? Has the seed of bitterness grown in the depths of their heart? Is there some form of satisfaction that comes from inflicting this same pain on someone else? Does it somehow avenge us of the wrongs that have been perpetrated against us?

Perhaps it gives them a false sense of power. The person who is being mistreated may feel powerless in the relationship. They may envy the power that the abuser appears to hold. Their unnatural desire for this power will allow them to justify repeating the negative behavior. It may help them to feel vindicated.

"But let him that glories glory in this, that he

understands and knows Me, that I am the LORD which exercise loving-kindness, judgment, and righteousness, in the earth: for in these things I delight", says the LORD.

Jeremiah 9:24 NIV

If we are seriously committed to our

relationship with Him, we will exalt Him above everyone and everything else in our lives. We will be totally and completely dedicated to living our lives for His honor. We will also be zealously committed to obeying His will for our lives. The primary goal of our lives will be to show the world that our God is the one true and living God.

People are designed to try to lead and to be led; some more than others. This inherent trait can cause problems. Sometimes people are quickly lining up to go along with those who appear to be leaders. It doesn't matter if the leader is self-proclaimed, nominated, hired or voted into office. They are often put on pedestals. The most devoted followers not only turn a blind eye to their shortcomings and misbehaviors, but they tolerate and justify them. People are willing to carry out certain tasks simply because someone in authority decrees it. This may seem like selfless devotion and many leaders crave this type of loyalty.

In reality, this devotion is often motivated by selfishness and deep seeded feelings of worthlessness. To be connected to someone who has a position of power gives them a sense of power. To maintain this

new-found sense of self-worth, they will often go to extreme levels. This includes burying their seeds of bitterness. These seeds won't stay buried indefinitely. The expressions of anger and bitterness will be repeated.

Until the Last Drop

The true Light who gives light to every man was coming into the world. He was in the world, and though the world was made through Him, the world did not recognize Him. He came to His own, and His own did not receive Him.

John 1:9-11

Today, I met a fly. He reminded me of a valuable lesson. When we find ourselves in difficult or seemingly impossible situations, we pray and cry, pray and cry. If we are deeply religious, we declare in GREAT faith, "I'm waiting for God to send me an answer. Anyway, He chooses to move, I'll be satisfied." Yet when God sends the answer, it often comes in ways that we are not expecting.

The Jews were waiting for and expecting the promised messiah. Yet when he came to speak peace and a message of love, they rejected him. The Jews rejected Jesus because, in their eyes, He failed to meet their expectations. He didn't do what they expected their Messiah to do. They were looking for a messiah to destroy evil and avenge them of all their enemies. They were looking for Him to establish an eternal earthly kingdom.

The prophecies of Isaiah 53 and Psalm 22 describe a suffering Messiah who would be persecuted and killed. It was clearly written in the sacred scriptures that they treasured. However, like many people today the Jews chose to focus on the prophecies that discuss His glorious victories. They chose to ignore His crucifixion.

The young lions do lack, and suffer hunger:
but they that seek the LORD
shall not want any good thing.
Psalm 34:10

When I met Mr. Fly, he was trapped inside of a jar. The jar had a very narrow opening at the top. Since the jar was made of clear acrylic, I was able to thoroughly observe him. He was struggling desperately to be released from his prison. He climbed all the way to the top of the jar multiple times but was unable to secure his freedom. In order to secure his freedom, he needed to fly through the very narrow slit in the top of the jar. There was only one other possibility for his escape. He would need to walk upside down across the underside of the top portion of the jar until he reached the opening. He was unable to master this trick.

If anyone has caused grief, he has not so much grieved me as he has grieved all of you to some extent—not to put it too severely. The punishment inflicted on him by the majority is sufficient. Now instead, you ought to forgive and comfort him, so that he will not be overwhelmed by excessive sorrow. I urge you, therefore, to reaffirm your love for him.

- 2 Corinthians 2:5-8 (NIV)

After watching him for approximately ten minutes, I decided to help him. Like so many others that I have attempted to rescue, he resisted. I shook the jar. He didn't come near the hole. Turning the jar upside down yielded no release for him. Turning the jar on each side provided no freedom for him. It seemed that he totally ignored the way of escape. However, I was determined that he was going to be free. Repeatedly, I flipped and turned the jar and he continued to ignore the way of escape.

Frustrated, I left the fly alone. It was so easy for him to go free. Why didn't he want to be free? Maybe, he wanted to be free, but he didn't want it bad enough. Maybe, he hadn't hit rock-bottom yet. He needed to get tired of being sick and tired. When was he going to learn? Was he institutionalized? What was his problem? This is not the way he was raised. He was born free.

Wait! I know what the problem is. I know this fly. I have tried too many times to set him free. He's just not ready yet. If he doesn't die in this prison, maybe one day he will be truly free.

Does this dialogue sound familiar? Does it sound comical? Have you ever found yourself in a similar situation? I have! It's too familiar to me. On more than one occasion, I have sought desperately to free someone from a dangerous or detrimental prison of the mind. I frustrated myself because they weren't ready.

In Him we have redemption through His blood, the forgiveness of our trespasses, according to the riches of His grace
Ephesians 1:7

After waiting for a while, I decided to offer the fly one last chance at redemption. I picked the jar up. As I barely tilted the jar, the fly flew out of the hole. He had decided that he wanted to be free.

Don't speak for me

When you feel the need to raise your voice in a
high pitched screech
Don't speak to me
Don't speak for me

When anger and bitterness determine your
speech
Don't speak to me
Don't speak for me

When envy and jealousy determine your tone
Don't speak to me
Don't speak for me

When there is no rhyme or reason for the words
you choose
Don't speak to me
Don't speak for me

When profanity seems to be your claim to fame
Don't speak to me
Don't speak for me

When bitterness seeks to bring me shame
Lord speak to me
Lord speak for me

Lest we Forget

All Scripture is *given by inspiration of God, and* is *profitable for doctrine, for reproof, for correction, for instruction in righteousness,* 2 Timothy 3:16 NKJV

Shortly after I met Buck in 1984, he went to prison. I was his co-defendant in that case. For those charges, I was sentenced to four years on probation. While Buck was in prison, I returned to a previous occupation, selling drugs.

Business was going well until Mama started dreaming again. She was always dreaming something about me. It was usually a warning for me to stop my negative behavior. I was starting to resent these dreams that exposed everything that I was trying to hide from her.

Mama called me one night and told me that she had dreamed that I was selling drugs. I assured her that she was severely mistaken. There was no way that I would ever stoop to selling drugs. She insisted on telling me that if I didn't stop what I was doing, I was going to be caught. This warning was familiar to me. This was the same warning that she gave me when I was stealing. This time, she was resolutely determined to acquire and maintain my undivided attention.

She said, "The police were searching your house. They were tearing your sofa apart; they were sure you had the dope inside of the sofa. They were tearing the foam in the back of the sofa into small pieces."

"Great peace have those who love your law; nothing can make them stumble."
Psalm 119:165 NIV

While I was assuring her that I would never stoop to selling drugs, at the same time, I was down on my knees in front of the sofa. The telephone was in my left hand and my right hand was reaching into the back of the sofa, pulling the marijuana from my hiding place. This was my hiding place that no one else knew about. That is except God. All I wanted was for her to hurry up and get off the telephone. She repeated her warnings several times, describing each detail of her dream. While she continued to repeat her warnings, it seemed like she was never going to let me get off the telephone.

She continued explaining, repeatedly, "The police were searching your house for drugs. They were so sure that you had the drugs; they were ripping your sofa to pieces. They were ripping the foam into small pieces."

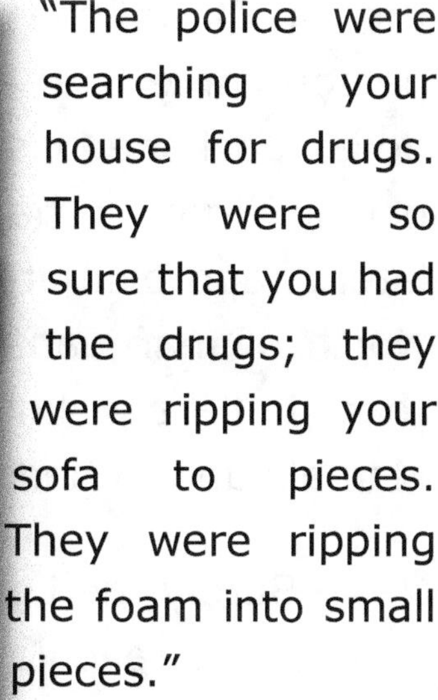

I was trying to remain calm, but I was afraid that the police would get there before she hung up the telephone. Mama never said anything that she considers important only once.

If something was really pressing on her mind, she would repeat the message until she got tired. I needed to get the dope out of the house before the police came. Finally, she was finished.

Nervously, I placed the drugs in a jar, rushed out of the house and quickly buried the drugs in the ground. When the next person came to the house requesting a five-dollar package, I suggested that he take all of the drugs I had and pay me for them later, approximately seventy-five dollars' worth of marijuana. This man was someone that I barely knew. That didn't matter; Mama's dream had me scared.

Surely the Lord God will do nothing but
He revealeth His secret unto
His servants the prophets.
Amos 3:7

All night long, I stayed awake, expecting the police to show up. Needless to say, I never was paid for the drugs, but that didn't matter. This could have been a seed of bitterness if I had allowed it to become one. Actually, I was so nervous that I don't remember his name. At least, the police hadn't found the dope.

For a few days, I was scared to sell anything. Then, the devil gave me another plan. He talked to me real good. Based on everything that had happened in the past, I was convinced that he was right. He told me that before anything happened to me, God would warn my mother and she would warn me. This was also greed talking to me. All I needed to do was find a new place to sell the drugs and avoid talking to my mother. As long as she was unable to talk to me, nothing would happen. This would keep me from getting caught selling drugs. This was a perfect plan.

Blessed [is] the man that endureth temptation: for when he is tried, he shall receive the crown of life, which the Lord hath promised to them that love him.

James 1:12 -

Two weeks after her warning, I went to see Denna, one of my former drug partners. Normally, she had a package of drugs, but currently, she didn't have anything.

She said, "Nobody brought anything by for me to sell."

She wanted to do something if I could work it out. She knew where I could get a pound of marijuana. We went to talk to her friend. The man didn't really know me, but he was familiar with my reputation. He was glad to give me the dope on credit. Thus, I set up shop at Denna's apartment. In addition to splitting the profits with her, I was also giving her part of the drugs for recreational use. I was too scared to go home with the dope; I would leave the drugs at her house each night, or should I say each morning. I went home each morning. This was long enough to take a nap, change clothes and get my daughter off to school. I went through all this trouble because I was afraid to talk to my mother.

I had a thriving small-time drug business. There was only one problem with my thriving business. Now, "Something" began to talk to me, regularly. I now called God, "Something." The voice constantly said, "You're going to get caught." Whenever I told anybody what the voice said to me, no one took me seriously. They assured me that I had been just paranoid because I had been snorting too much cocaine.

Put on the whole armour of God, that ye may be able to stand against the wiles of the devil.
Ephesians 6:11

There were times when I would sit on the train tracks paranoid. I was trying to see if I could locate the policemen that were watching the house. Sometimes, I would walk over into the woods and frantically bury the dope. Other times, while I was riding down the street, I would sling the dope out the car window in a brown paper bag, just like trash. When someone would come to make a purchase, I would go back to where I had thrown the drugs from the car. Sometimes, I couldn't even locate the bag, but this wouldn't stop me from repeating the pattern. Whenever I went to the shopping center, this has always been my pattern. The voice became more frequent and more insistent, "You're going to get caught." There was no doubt in my mind where the voice was coming from, but I wasn't going to admit that I knew the source.

"I have heard a report from the Lord..."
Jeremiah 49:14, AMP

Finally, I told Denna that I was going to stop selling drugs. The fear of being caught with the drugs had become overwhelming. Denna told me that she had several bills that hadn't been paid for the month. I agreed to get one more package to help her out of her situation. For more than a week, our source was out of drugs and we were waiting for him to re-up (get a new shipment). We continuously told our customers to check back later, not knowing exactly when we would get the new supply. This went on for several days. There was one regular customer who had requested that I give him a tester when I got the new supply of cocaine. Pete was a good and regular customer and so I agreed. After making several trips that week to pick up the drugs and coming back without them, I was finally able to pick up the package. This was directly against everything going on in my mind. Within ten minutes of my returning to the house with the drugs, things would go quickly downhill.

Going directly to the back bedroom, I quickly began to do three things at once. Placing all the drugs on the bed, I began to prepare the packages. I poured the cocaine on a mirror. There was one person waiting for an ounce of marijuana and Pete was waiting for the tester. I prepared both of these, gave Denna the package to sell and Pete the tester. He went into the bathroom to get off, taking drugs intravenously. Once I went back to work breaking down the drugs, I heard the voice of "Something" speak again.

He said, "The police are in the house."

There was no doubt in my mind what

was happening in the house. I had given Denna a code to use if anything ever went wrong, but she didn't say a word. If she had warned me, it wouldn't have helped. Scraping the cocaine from the mirror, I hurriedly put the drug back into the zip-lock bag. I put the marijuana into a shopping bag. There was no way to hide two pounds of marijuana. I quickly moved to stand behind the door. Standing behind the door, I placed the zip-lock bag of cocaine inside my clothes.

While I was standing behind the door, a policeman knocked on the bedroom door and identified himself. Before the door could be opened, I needed to move from behind it. He allowed me time to move. When he entered the room, he instructed me to go into the living room to sit down with the other people in the house. Pete was caught in the bathroom with his syringe.

Although I remember three of the officer's names that raided the house clearly, I won't identify them. The first reason being, one agreed to let me go to the bathroom. He didn't know it, but this gave me a chance to secure the cocaine more completely. The second reason being that by the time the marijuana was weighed and the charges made, several ounces of the drug were missing. Stranger yet, the person who had just bought the ounce of marijuana was allowed to leave the house immediately. This could have caused another seed of bitterness. Denna's mother, her father, and her boyfriend were also in the house. Her parents would eventually be allowed to leave.

But now you must put them all away: anger,

wrath, malice, slander, and obscene talk from
your mouth. Put on then, as God's chosen ones,
holy and beloved, compassionate hearts,
kindness, humility, meekness, and patience,
bearing with one another and, if one has a
complaint against another, forgiving each other;
as the Lord has forgiven you,
so you also must forgive.
Colossians 3:8, 12-13

The detectives had failed to produce a search warrant; therefore, I began to request that one be produced. They told me that this was not my house. I was hoping Denna would follow-up on this question, but she didn't. No warrant was ever produced.

The detectives brought the shopping bag of marijuana out of the bedroom and began to discuss who would be charged. They explained to Denna that since this was her house, she was definitely being charged. They asked her if she wanted to make any statement at this time. She made none. Waiting, I hoped that she would at least say let everybody else go. We could help her more if we were free. She remained silent. This was dumbfounding to me since the possession of cocaine was a more severe charge. This could have been another seed of bitterness.

"Now may the Lord of peace himself give you peace at all times in every way.

2 Thessalonians 3:16

The detectives decided to arrest the four people remaining in the house. As we were escorted from the house, the neighbors were outside watching. The embarrassment could have led to the seeds of bitterness.

Denna and I both received prison sentences for the charges we received that day. There were actually two people named Pete in the house on that day. One of them was the person who introduced me to Buck. We remained friends until his death several years ago. The second Pete agreed to testify in court about how generous I had been to give him the tester. The sarcasm is intentional. I never saw him again. He was brutally murdered several years ago. It gave me no satisfaction. Lord, forgive me and remove the seeds of bitterness that have remained.

Refrain from anger and turn from wrath; do not fret—it leads only to evil.
For those who are evil will be destroyed,
but those who hope in the LORD

will inherit the land.

Psalm 37:8-9 NIV

Denna's parents were also in the home that day. They weren't arrested, but both were considered material witnesses to be available for a possible trial. Denna's mother wanted to protect her daughter and prevent her from going to jail.

Denna and I were both on probation. My probation officer had warned me that if I were ever arrested for drugs, he would recommend violating my probation. Her probation officer was a younger man and based on her description, I was sure that he would be easier to manipulate. Sitting in the cell, I began to prepare one plan for Denna and one for me.

Immediately upon my release, I would begin working my plan, careful to follow every detail. The first step was to get Denna out before her probation officer found out about the arrests for Possession of Narcotics. She was on probation for the same type of offense. The night that I got out, I was about twenty dollars short of the money for Denna's bail. I went to her family for help, but they wouldn't even help me with this small amount of money to secure her freedom. I was able to get her out the next day.

I was able to move forward with my plan to ensure my probation officer wasn't going to lock me up. I needed to be the first person to tell him about my arrest. When I went to see him, I took with me a stack of letters from people in the community and some professional agencies about how I had helped them. The letters were true. My plan came off better than I anticipated and resulted in me being allowed to remain out on bail until he received the police report. He would make a final decision after reviewing this report.

Denna, however, decided not to follow the plan I had given her. She had a probation officer that was a young Black man and he was new to the profession. Realizing that these should work in her favor, I told her to wear a provocative dress and to go in begging for mercy. I told her to tell him that she would do anything to stay free, but to be careful not to proposition him. She decided not to talk to her probation officer. Once, he found out about the charges, he issued a warrant for her arrest. It was only then that she wanted my help.

She called me and said, "My probation officer has issued a warrant for my arrest. What should I do now?"

I asked her why she hadn't gone to see him.

She said, "I didn't have time."

I knew that once the warrant had been issued, this had to be served; she had to be arrested. There was nothing that I could do to stop the process.

The next day, when she went to see the probation officer, he locked the door and called the police to pick her up. Her brother called me to tell me what had happened to her.

Be not deceived; God is not mocked: for whatsoever a man soweth, that shall he also reap.

For he that soweth to his flesh shall of the flesh reap corruption; but he that soweth to the Spirit shall of the Spirit reap life everlasting.

Galatians 6:7-8

He stated, "Denna asked them what they were going to do about you. The probation officer explained to her that you weren't on his caseload and he didn't have anything to do with you."

"Peace I leave with you; my peace I give to you. Not as the world gives do I give to you. Let not your hearts be troubled,
neither let them be afraid."

John 14:27

I couldn't understand why she was asking about me, but this troubled me and was a dangerous warning sign. She knew that I had already reported to my probation officer what had happened.

After the police report came back and my probation officer received the report, he called me and told me that I would need to turn myself into the Sheriff's Department at the Government Center. My probation hearing was scheduled for that Friday. I relayed this information to my attorney and arrangements were made for me to turn myself in at 3:00 p.m., accompanied by my attorney.

When my lawyer and I arrived at the Sheriff's Department, the sheriff deputies searched, but they didn't have a warrant for my arrest. My attorney called my probation officer and he said that he was bringing the warrant. As the Sheriff's Department was located directly across from the District Attorney's Office, my attorney suggested that we go and ask the DA if he would be willing to let me remain free until the day of the probation hearing. This hearing would be necessary to determine if I had violated my probation. The District Attorney agreed to see us and to my shock seemed to consider the request. When my probation officer arrived, the DA asked for his personal recommendation.

"I don't have one. I told her that if she ever had a problem with drugs, I would recommend that she be locked up."

The DA requested to see my probation officer in private. Speechless, within myself, I prayed and held my breath at the same time. When they returned, they told me something that I could believe. I was still free. The probation hearing was scheduled for the end of the week. I could remain free until the hearing.

That Friday, a probation hearing was held to determine my immediate fate. At my hearing, the detectives testified that the apartment was under surveillance for several weeks. They stated that they had never seen me at the apartment before. One of these statements had to be a lie, but I had been there every day for months. However, this worked in my favor. I wasn't about to correct them. My probation officer also reluctantly testified at this hearing. He tried to avoid making a statement, but the judge insisted that he make a recommendation.

"You have had more contact with her

than anybody else. What do you know about her?"

Till I make thine enemies thy footstool.
Luke 20:43

With no choice left, he said, "She's paid her fees on time each month. She reports when she is scheduled. Sometimes, her children come to the office with her. The children are clean and well behaved. It appears that she takes good care of them."

No one else was allowed to testify. Denna's mother was angry she wanted to testify to make sure they locked me up with her daughter. This was in spite of the fact that I did many things to help her and her daughter. She kept waving her hand for the judge to recognize her, but he never did. Her father, however, said if they asked him any questions, he was going to speak the truth.

At the end of the hearing, I was placed on intensive probation. This meant that I now had a 10:00 p.m. curfew. Several times a week, two armed officers would verify that

I complying with these conditions. This was embarrassing because the neighbors observed them coming to my house, but the only other option was even more embarrassing. Additionally, I was given community service hours to complete. These hours were completed in one week. I wanted to get this out of the way. I was also required to report to the probation office several times a month. These requirements were a small price to pay for my freedom.

God is a righteous judge, a God who displays his wrath every day.Psalm 7:11 NIV

There was plenty opportunity for seeds of bitterness to grow. Was I bitter? No! I was too afraid of my future to be angry or bitter. I needed a miracle and I knew who ultimately held my freedom in His hands. It was time for me to give my life back to God.

After our release from prison, we never spoke of this time in our lives. I continued to maintain a relationship with Denna's family. I understood how her mother felt. Rather than focus on bitterness, I chose to focus on how good she could cook. She had made me welcome at her table on numerous occasions.

She was in the hospital prior to her death a few years ago. The grace of God allowed me to be making visits on the same floor in the hospital. Each time, I saw a member of her family. I was able to spend time with her before she passed. Denna's father has also passed.

Today I was reading the obituaries in our local paper. I saw a name that looked vaguely familiar to me. Immediately, I went to social media to aid me in identifying her. To my shock, it was the person who bought the ounce of marijuana from me that day. When she began purchasing drugs from me, it didn't feel right. Her father was a known drug dealer. He had a business relationship with the person who I was purchasing drugs from. Why wasn't she buying from her father? I chose to ignore these feelings.

A thief's partner is his own worst enemy. He will

be punished if he tells the truth in court, and
God will curse him if he doesn't.
Proverbs 29:24 GNB

That final day, she arrived thirty minutes early for the purchase. Earlier in the day, she had been given a designated time to pick the package up. Her arrival interrupted my schedule. There wasn't enough time for me to sort the drugs and hide them. When the police knocked on the door of the home, she threw the bag of drugs that she had purchased down. She was immediately allowed to leave the home without explanation. I was certain that she played a part in our arrest.

As far as I know, I never saw her after that day. If I did, I didn't recognize her. In the beginning, I wished her ill and I thank God for the grace that protected me from my foolishness. No seeds of bitterness are here.

I know

I know my place.
I know that children are to be seen and not heard.
I know not to talk back to my elders.
I know to keep my nose out of grown folks business.
I know not to talk back to my elders.
I know to say, "Yes ma'am and no ma'am."
I know my place. I know not to question adults.
I know to be thankful for whatever I get.
I know to say, "Please".
I know to say, "Thank you."
I know to say, "Excuse me please."
I know when to say, "I'm sorry."
I know to say grace before I eat.
I know to bow my head before I sleep.
I know to eat all the food on my plate because there are hungry children in the world.
I know that I shouldn't talk with food in my mouth.

I know to cover my mouth when I cough.
Believe me, this child knows her place.
I know that if you get out of your place, it may
mean a backhand slap across your face
And it's not called child abuse.
It didn't leave bruises and there were no trips to
the hospital.
I know that was then
and this is now.
I know.
I really do know.

It's Mine

"There is neither evil nor transgression

in my hand,

1 Samuel 24:11

One of the first phrases that a child learns is, "It's mine" or "Mine." This selfish nature is inbred in us from the time we are born, life becomes a struggle to obtain and maintain the things that we believe belong to us. The problem arises when we confuse a privilege with a right to have something.

When we begin to have feelings of entitlement, it often leads to bitterness.

Dysfunctional families have many secrets. They will go to extreme lengths to keep the family secrets. The fear of their secrets being exposed may be the greatest motivating factor for their behavior. Every family has some secrets or things that they consider private family business. Dysfunctional families have generational secrets that are maintained.

There was a woman that I knew. To simplify the story, we will call her Miss Martha. She had at least seven children. The children may have had as many as six different fathers. We will never know. She had secrets.

For the Lord will not reject forever, For if He causes grief, Then He will have compassion According to His abundant lovingkindness.
Lamentations 3:31-32 NAS

As the children grew older, they began to ask questions about their fathers. One of

Miss Martha's children was raised by his father's family. This later became a source of pain to that child. He never understood why Miss Martha had given him away and kept the others. It was a seed of bitterness for him. Actually, he may have fared better than the other children. What he perceived as a negative worked out for his good.

Miss Martha never married. She was raised in a home with her mother and father, Sarah and Larry Grant. At various times, other family members also lived in the home. After Larry's death, Miss Martha and Sarah continued to live together. Sarah was blessed with long life. She lived to be over a hundred years old. Miss Sarah and her husband, Larry, were born slaves.

Miss Martha's older children report that their youngest sibling, Sandy, was born at home. They never knew that their mother was pregnant. According to their memories, one day, they heard the sound of crying coming from the bedroom. The sound reminded them of a cat. They thought there was a cat in the bedroom. It was at that point that they learned about the new addition to the family.

It might seem that Miss Martha was a very promiscuous woman, but the other things about her character suggest this was not the case. She worked hard to provide for her children. Miss Martha worked as a domestic aide, nanny, and cook for several prominent families in the community. She maintained a close relationship with these families throughout her life. She often earned extra money by ironing in her home for other people. She kept her children and her house clean. She was a religious woman and active supporter of her church. She was not a consumer of strong drink or alcoholic beverages. She didn't smoke or dip snuff. She was never reported to be a woman who frequented nightclubs or bars. Her children didn't meet new uncles (boyfriends) on a regular basis.

The older children had no indication of who fathered the younger siblings. The father of the two youngest children was later identified. Most of the older children never learned the identity of their fathers.

Miss Martha never married or expressed any regrets. She wasn't a bitter woman. The seeds of bitterness were not apparent in her life. She wasn't known for being angry or raising her voice. She wasn't known for being a big gossiper. She was never accused of verbally or physically abusing her children. Actually, Miss Martha's mother was the disciplinarian for the children. Miss Martha never used harsh or profane words. This is not to imply that her children found no fault in her.

Miss Martha was often accused of showing extreme favoritism among her children. It seemed that she was almost indifferent to some of them. While Miss Martha was not abusive to her children, her treatment of some of them bordered on emotional neglect. These same feelings reflected in the way she treated her grandchildren. The favoritism was so obvious that the children she favored often resented Miss Martha's apparent lack of emotions toward the other siblings.

Fathers, do not provoke your children, lest they become discouraged.

Colossians 3:21

Did this cause the seeds of resentment? Yes, it did. It bothered each of her children in different ways. Those who received the favoritism were uncomfortable. Her youngest child, Sandy, was her favorite child. This child knew that this hurt her siblings and she loved her brothers and sisters. On numerous occasions, she told Miss Martha that it just wasn't right. The way Sandy expressed this to Miss Martha wasn't right either. Her words were laced with bitterness.

"So whatever you wish that others would do to you, do also to them, for this is the Law and the Prophets.

Matthew 7:12

Oddly, no one resented Sandy or her child. She was everyone's favorite sibling.

She was the most colorful of the siblings. She was also everyone's favorite relative. She was the glue that held the family together. She was a great entertainer, comedian, compassionate, and generous. She would shift the atmosphere of any room that she entered.

When Sandy married, the favoritism caused problems in her marriage. Her husband resented the way Miss Martha treated his wife and child. Miss Martha was always buying things for them.

One Christmas, Miss Martha splurged on Christmas for her favorite grandchild. The gifts included clothes, a television, and anything else she thought the child might want. She had many grandchildren and she didn't forget them. She gave one of her other grandchildren $2 to purchase Christmas stockings for the other children at a nearby grocery store. Each of the stockings cost a dime. Yes, there were seeds of bitterness in the heart of more than one person.

Give thanks in all circumstances; for this is the

will of God in Christ Jesus for you.

1 Thessalonians 5:18 ESV

It would have been disrespectful for the grandchild to tell Miss Martha how she felt. She carefully obeyed the instructions and hid her tears. If she had confronted her grandmother, Miss Martha wouldn't have responded. Another type of grandmother would have said, "This is my money. I worked for it, it's mine! I'll spend it any way I like! I don't owe you anything!"

Miss Martha's mother was known by her children and grandchildren, as Mama. It was Mama's role to provide the love and nurturing that the children needed. After Mama's death, the family gatherings centered on Sandy coming home for a visit. When Miss Martha passed, the family gatherings became rare and almost non-existent.

A fool's lips enter into contention,

and his mouth calleth for strokes.

Proverbs 18:6

During Miss Martha's later years, one of her elderly neighbors accused her of lying. She didn't argue with the woman. She was so upset that she called the police.

When the officer arrived, he asked, "Can you tell me exactly what she said to you?"

Struggling for words, Miss Martha replied, "She called me something that means I was telling a story!"

Again, the officer sought clarification, "What exactly did she say?"

Miss Martha attempted to explain. She wanted the woman punished, but could not allow herself to say the word. It would have been disrespectful for me to tell him what she was trying not to say. As he drove away, the police officer must have been laughing. Standing nearby watching the incident, I was doing exactly that, laughing.

I have cared for you since you were
born. Yes, I carried you before you
were born. I will be your God
throughout your lifetime—until your

hair is white with age. I made you, and I will care for you. I will carry you along and save you.

Isaiah 46:3b-4 NLT

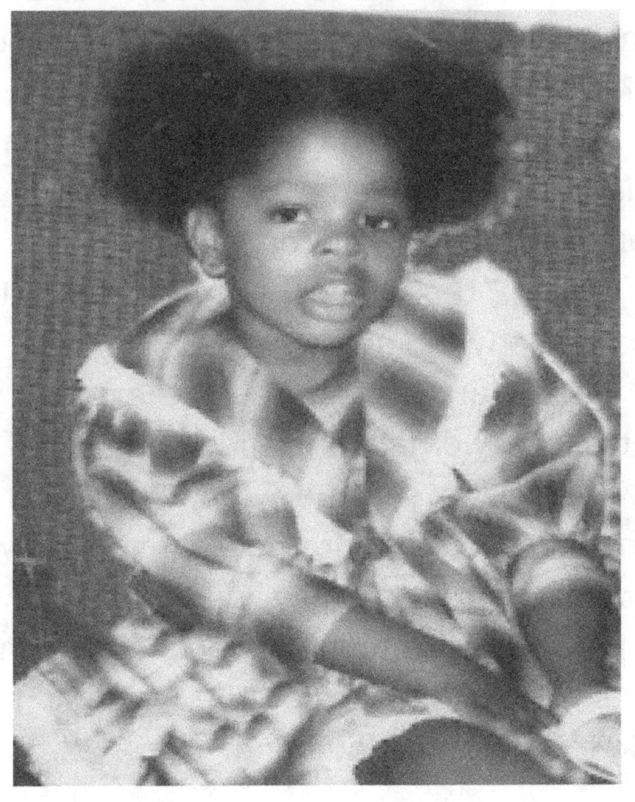

Although Miss Martha lived to be almost ninety-years-old, she never discussed her secrets. She took the secrets to her grave. There were many rumors, the mailman, the son of people that she worked for, the milkman, etc. Her descendants will never know the truth. Those who may have had some clues chose to keep the secrets. They too have now passed on.

Miss Martha had many relatives that lived in the home with her during that time. For some reason, they didn't know the answers or chose not to share them. Future generations will ask the same questions that have been asked before, but no answers will come. The answers were buried a long time ago. They were buried years before Miss Martha was buried at Green Acres Cemetery in Columbus, Georgia. They were buried in her heart.

I wonder if there was a reason that Miss Martha protected her secrets. I ask myself if the way that she treated her children was a reflection of her feelings for their fathers. She was born during a time when some subjects were taboo. Some things were kept hidden. They were kept secret. Perhaps her secrets were too painful to share. Miss Martha's story may be a common story. These seeds of bitterness are common.

Do not be anxious about anything, but in everything by prayer and supplication with thanksgiving let your requests be made known to God.
Philippians 4:6

During my hospital stay at Grady, Sandy was the first to arrive at the hospital. Although I couldn't see myself clearly, I was worried about how it would affect my mother to see me in this condition. They had told me she was on her way to the hospital. When Mama arrived, Sandy entered the room with her. I was still wondering about how this would affect my mother. Immediately, I began to apologize to her for putting her through this crisis. She assured me that she was glad that God had spared her to be there for me. Consistently she repeated, "I thank God that He allowed me the chance to be here for you."

While Mama was being serious, Sandy, the person who was going to become her constant companion had other plans. She is a real comedian and she wanted me to laugh. She told me that when she was told about what had happened to me, she ran to the car. There was only one problem. She was running so fast that she missed the car. She slid up under the car and had to be pulled from under it. She had been drinking, but she was sober now. This would begin a continuous routine of them visiting me.

These two people would be the only ones to weather the storm. Mama spent five days in Atlanta, on her first visit, before returning to Columbus and returned every weekend to visit me during the remainder of my stay in the hospital. When she went back to Columbus the first time, she took Earline back with her, to live with Ma'Dear.

Sandy came several times a day, for almost three months until the nurses asked her to skip a day. They said that I was getting too dependent on her. She was there for each of her siblings in their time of need. There were no seeds of bitterness for the baby in the family.

Enough to go Around

"In your anger do not sin": Do not let the sun go down while you are still angry,

Ephesians 4:26 (NIV)

There is enough bitterness to go around. Everyone is affected by bitterness. Each of us has endured our own battles with bitterness. It can be a minor irritation or it can become severe enough to cause someone to contemplate murder or suicide. When bitterness becomes severe, it will affect every area of your life. It also affects those who encounter the person consumed with bitterness.

It can be a temporary problem which is soon resolved. When bitterness is uprooted quickly, it lessens the chances of the infection spreading. When it becomes a long-term problem, it can be difficult if not impossible to overcome. It leads a wide array of destructive conditions. Bitterness negatively affects every area of our physical, emotional, mental, social, and spiritual well-being.

But the fearful, and unbelieving, and the abominable, and murderers, and whoremongers, and sorcerers, and idolaters, and all liars, shall have their part in the lake which burneth with fire and brimstone: which is the second death.
Revelation 21:8

Just as a lesser sin leads to greater sin, a bitter seed can lead to a full grown tree of bitterness. People usually think of lesser sins as nothing more serious than a "lil' white lie." The Bible teaches us to maintain our fear of God (reverence of God) and hatred of sin. The Bible clearly states the destination for all liars, the Lake of Fire.

If we begin to look into our own hearts, it is probable that we will find some seeds of bitterness. Some may be great others may be small. There are times when we, too, are resistant to the change that Christ seeks to work within us.

We can easily find excuses to exempt ourselves from submitting to the will of God and the transformation offered in the gospel. We attempt to rationalize our disobedience to God's Word and the convicting power of the Holy Spirit.

But now you must also rid yourselves of all such things as these: anger, rage, malice, slander, and filthy language from your lips.

Colossians 3:8 NIV

Sometimes, we believe that we have overcome anger and bitterness. Yet, every time their very name is brought up, the pain returns as if it happened yesterday. Even if it was years ago when it occurred, the thought of what occurred continue to bring back the pain associated with the transgression. Just thinking of them, your heart rate increases and your blood pressure begins to rise. When you think about what they said or did, you begin to relive the pain. It's as though you were reliving it over again, just thinking about it!

There was an elderly woman, Mother Gray, who I loved deeply and respected her. In many ways, I considered her a spiritual mother. She seemed to be the very epitome of the virtuous woman in Proverbs. She had been saved for numerous years. She was dedicated to her local church and active in ministry. She did many good deeds and was known for her generosity. I admired her greatly.

Do not be quickly provoked in your spirit, for

anger resides in the lap of fools.

Ecclesiastes 7:9 NIV

One day, something happened to hurt Mother Gray to the core of being. There were several versions of what happened. I do not know the full truth of what precipitated the series of events. Something that she treasured was taken from her. She was offended. She became angry and almost immediately bitter. The seeds of bitterness were so strong that they affected the church.

It marred the sweetness that she once exuded. In her presence, there was no fullness of joy. It had been replaced. There was the fullness of bitterness.

The very mention of the name of the person with whom she associated this grievous pain caused her lips to tremble. She talked about this perceived wrong often at church. The spirit of bitterness was so strong that it made others uncomfortable.

So the LORD was very angry with Israel and
removed them from his presence.
Only the tribe of Judah was left,
2 Kings 17:18 NIV

A church without the presence and anointing of God is just a building. One Sunday, the pastor and a portion of the membership were absent from the morning worship service. There were a few visitors present. Most of the people present had been affected with second-hand bitterness. Because of their great love for her, they became bitter too. The service is one that I have been unable to forget. It was the first and hopefully the last time I will be in a church service almost completely devoid of the presence of God.

Enter his gates with thanksgiving, and his courts with praise! Give thanks to him; bless his name!
Psalm 100:4 ESV

Mother Gray was the speaker for the occasion. Halfway through the service, one of the visitors stood up. As she headed hastily for the door, she was heard saying, "I didn't come here for that!"

because human anger does not produce the righteousness that God desires.
James 1:20 NIV

This open bitterness continued for months. It hurt me deeply to see her in so much pain. It hurt, even more, to see her destroying her Christian testimony. One night, I dreamed about Mother Gray. By the grace of God, I was given the opportunity to talk to talk to her. She brought the subject up. She was older than my mother; this made me careful to respond to her. She had been saved a lot longer than I had and I didn't feel qualified to give her the message of forgiveness that God had given me for her. Yet, I had been heavy from the weight of the message.

Fools give full vent to their rage,
but the wise bring calm in the end.
Proverbs 29:11 NIV

There was a long silence before I mustered the courage to speak. Before I uttered three words, Mother Gray's lips began to quiver and she began to stutter. She attempted to cut me off, but someone else in the room intervened. As I continued with the message, she bitterly protested, "I have forgiven him. It's just..." When the conversation was over, her bottom lip was still quivering. I pray that she was able to forgive him.

In my Mirror
I-C-U

When I look in my mirror
What do I see?
When I'm ready to make corrections
I don't see me
I-C-U

Call me tired and lazy
Well, I looked in my mirror
All ready to make corrections
I don't see me
I-C-U

Call me bitter and hateful
Again, I looked in my mirror
Ready for the corrections
I don't see me+-
I-C-U

Call me the loathsome kind

Where's my mirror
This just can't be
When I look in my mirror
I just don't see me
It's you that I see

Seed of Forgiveness

"Be not angry that you cannot make others as you wish them to be since you cannot make yourself as you wish to be."

~ Thomas A' Kempis

A number of years ago, I was interviewed about my first book. Prior to taping the show, my mother and I spent some time with the host. The host had just finished reading *A Journey to Hell and Back*. Something about my relationship with my ex-husband, Robert, triggered a negative memory in her life.

Angrily, she said, "I hate Robert! I just hate him!"

Mama interrupted her, "No! No! I love him!"

How could my mother make this

statement? It's the truth! While I was still in intensive care, Robert brought food to the hospital for Mama to eat. One person asked her how she was able to eat it, knowing that domestic violence was directly responsible for my plight.

Mama responded, "I am not trying to go to hell! It's by God's grace! I'm not going to let anybody make me hate them!" Mama was rejecting the seeds of bitterness.

Before I was released from the hospital, psychiatrists met with me. Later, they met with Mama. They were concerned about my ability to cope with the trauma. They were also concerned with Mama's ability to cope with the stress of my recovery.

But the fruit of the Spirit is love, joy, peace, patience, kindness, goodness, faithfulness, gentleness, self-control; against such things there is no law. And those who belong to Christ Jesus have crucified the flesh with its passions and desires. If we live by the Spirit, *let us also walk by the Spirit.*

Galatians 5:22-25

Mama assured them, "It will not be a burden for me! I thank God that He allowed me to be here when my child needs me."

Each of us has good qualities and bad qualities. When people read my first book, they often have negative feelings about Robert. However, I chose not to let the seeds of bitterness grow in my heart towards him. How was this possible? It was the grace of God.

I have many painful memories of that relationship. There are no real memories of the marriage. It is difficult for me to imagine that I did marry him. Today, I consider Robert a friend. There is very little that he wouldn't do for me. My choice to forgive Robert was the right one.

And He said unto me, Son of man, can these bones live? And I answered, O Lord GOD, thou knowest.

Ezekiel 37:3

When I was at the point of death, my salvation became more important than revenge. If God was willing to forgive me, I needed to forgive Robert. Anger and bitterness would have delayed my recovery. I allowed God to pour the oil of forgiveness into my wounds.

When I asked Earline about her feelings for Robert, she was reluctant to discuss them. She was there on that near-fatal day. She was four-years-old at the time. She had no understanding of hate. She didn't fully understand what had happened. Therefore, she did not assign any malice to Robert. Years later, she began to understand why other people were angry with him about that day. She was confused and uncomfortable talking about it. Yet, she continued to reject the seeds of bitterness.

When I wrote my first book, my family was provided the opportunity to read it prior to publication. Prior to that time, I had never discussed the abuse with anyone other than Mama and my husband, Buck. It was not my desire to breed hatred or bitterness in my children. Therefore, I didn't discuss this painful information with them. No one else was allowed to discuss it with them.

And it shall come to pass, when your children shall say unto you, What mean ye by this service? Exodus 12:26

Earline has always loved Robert. After reading the book, Earline would not allow anyone to talk to her in detail about that day. She was uncomfortable when other people wanted to discuss it in detail. She hates the words, burned up.

Earline does not express anger, resentment, or bitterness towards Robert. She always treated him with respect and love. She remembers him as being a good father figure and treating her as if she were his own child. Earline knows his problems. She has chosen the high road, the seeds of forgiveness.

But if ye will not hear it, my soul shall weep in secret places for your pride; and mine eye shall weep sore, and run down with tears, because the LORD'S flock is carried away captive.
Jeremiah 13:17

After being confused about that day for so long, she finds it difficult to assign feelings to it now. For years, she had feelings of guilt. She blamed herself for what happened that day. When the fighting started, I sent her next door to the neighbor's apartment. The neighbors had a big boulder constrictor. She was angry at having to be in the house with the snake.

Instead, I have calmed and quieted myself, like a weaned child who no longer cries for its mother's milk. Yes, like a weaned child is my soul within me.

Psalm 131:2 NLT

Thinking the fighting had ended, she slipped quietly back into the apartment. After hearing the fighting was ongoing, Earline went back to her room to complete her schoolwork. She remembers being in her bedroom and seeing me pass by quickly and noticing something burning in the bathroom. Earline decided to see what was happening. She saw the paper burning in the bathroom. It looked like a little fire, but she couldn't understand why we didn't put it out. Earline thought about attempting to extinguish the fire. She knew that if you were on fire, you should stop, drop, and roll.

Be strong and courageous. Do not be terrified; do not be discouraged, for the Lord your God will be with you wherever you go.

Joshua 1:9 NIV

After hearing a sound from the bedroom, Earline became scared and ran out the apartment. She decided the fire department needed to be called. She rushed back to the neighbor's apartment. She asked the neighbor to call them. She was terrified something was wrong inside the bedroom.

The neighbor wouldn't let her out of the apartment the second time. The neighbor later told her that I would not be able to take care of her and that I was going to the hospital. She asked Earline for a telephone number to contact someone in her family. Initially, she was too nervous to remember the numbers. Eventually, she gave her the number for her grandmother in Columbus, Georgia.

Somehow, a family member took Earline to the hospital. She wasn't allowed to see me. At some point, police officers interviewed her. When she got older, she blamed herself for Robert not being arrested. She had told the police officer that she saw me throw the paper into the bathroom. She told them it was an accident; she assumed that the house had caught fire. At the hospital, she saw Robert walk into the room.

His hair was white. She thought he had been so scared that his hair turned white or ashes made his hair turn white.

Refrain from anger, and forsake wrath!

Fret not yourself; it tends only to evil.

Psalms 37:8

My Aunt Bobbie was angry that Robert was at the hospital. Earline remembers that my mother was just scared; she was trying to get my aunt to calm down and focus on what was important, my life. Earline thought it was an accident. My aunt didn't want to hear that. She was convinced that she knew what had happened. On one occasion, she had been on the phone with me when Robert beat me.

Earline didn't see me again until I returned home from the hospital, over three months later. She was surprised that I was so sick. No one had bothered to explain this to her. She assumed that when I came home, I would be well. For most of my life, my family subscribed to a philosophy that children should be seen and not heard. Adult problems weren't discussed with children. Eventually, Mama explained to Earline that I would have to learn how to walk and how to do other things again.

Until Earline read the draft of *A Journey to Hell and Back*, she harbored feelings of confusion and guilt. She blamed herself for the arguments and not putting the fire out. Because of her feelings of guilt, her other feelings towards Robert were confused. She believes that it was also hard for Robert to deal with what happened that day and that he has unexpressed remorse.

Earline feels that his generosity is his way of apologizing. Although he has never stated the specific reason for his remorse to her, his continued financial and emotional support indicates to her that he regretted that day. It is her opinion that he regretted the fire. She believes that his stating to her that he made mistakes in the marriage and with me is his expression of remorse without talking about a difficult subject.

Robert taught Earline how to cook, gave her a love for reading by encouraging her to read one page from the dictionary each day, encouraged her academic success, moved her into her first apartment, visited her when I was in prison and remained in her life following the divorce from me. She is not blind to his past, his frailty, weakness, and humanity, but she also sees his love.

Earline doesn't understand how bad things come from good people. Yet, she understands that sin is the culprit. Without God, a man left to his own devices will do anything. She sees Robert as a man who has been unable to live life on life's terms. When looking back on her own mistakes, it helps her to be more tolerant of others.

There are "friends" who destroy each other but a real friend sticks closer than a brother.

Proverbs 18:24 NLT

After reading the draft of the book, Herman was angry and bitter. He chose to medicate these feelings. He didn't know with whom he could discuss his wounds. Herman began to feel bitterness and resentment towards all men. He later realized that my mother and I had forgiven Robert. This gave him the desire to want to forgive him, too.

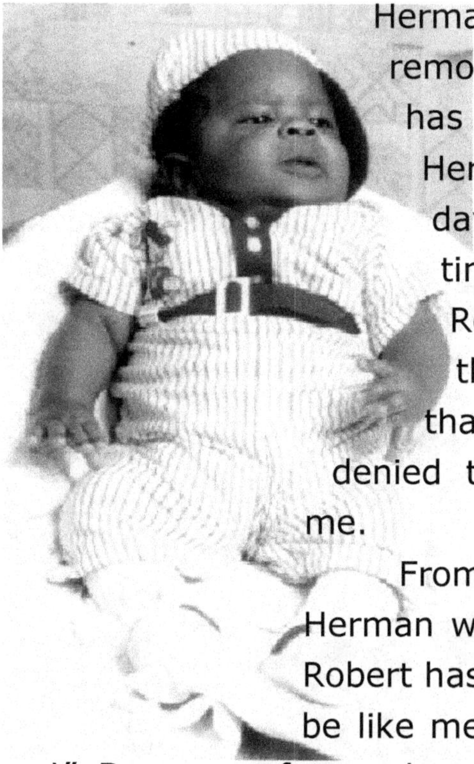

Herman says he sees remorse in Robert. He has talked to Herman about that day a couple of times. Once, Robert cried as they discussed that day. Robert denied that he ever hit me.

From the time Herman was a small child, Robert has told him, "Don't be like me! Be better than me!" Because of my abuse, Herman takes extra care to be charming. He always tries to be a gentleman and considerate. As a child, he made a vow to himself that he would never beat his wife. Most of the women Herman meets have experienced some form of physical, verbal, spiritual, or sexual abuse.

Herman was raised around many women. He has received lots of affection from women in the family, the neighborhood, the church, the schools, and my friends. Herman feels that being raised around so many women makes him highly attentive to their wounds and causes him to spread himself too thin, at times. Because he has met so many women who have been wounded and scorned by men, he feels an obligation to show them that "all men aren't the same." His efforts to go out of his way at being charming are his way of compensating for the damage done by his father.

Many women often assume that Herman's attention, affection, and empathy are synonymous with a romantic interest. He flirts with most of the women he meets. This flirtation has little to do with physical appearance; he does not discriminate. He has been a flirt most of his life.

My uncle started this habit. As a toddler, my uncle would take Herman with him when he was on the prowl for women.

Uncle T said, "I take him with me to help me catch! When he's walking around, they stop and say, 'Look at him. He's so short and cute.' That's all it takes!"

Herman likes to make all women feel valued. He is overprotective of all the women who he loves. From the time, he was about seven years old, adult women began sharing their personal problems with him. He is a compassionate listener and friend. He has provided sound Biblical advice.

A man's discretion makes him slow to anger, And it is his glory to overlook a transgression.
Proverbs 19:11 NAS

Before reading the draft of my first book, Herman was vaguely aware of how I had been burned. Herman remembers one day as I was applying the rod of correction, he screamed that he wanted his father. He states, "You stopped whipping me and asked me if I knew how you had been burned. All you said to me was that it was my father's fault." Although he may have wondered what that meant, he

never asked. As a small child, Herman didn't know that I had been burned. He assumed that I was born this way. Over the years, people have tried to tell him what happened. He acted as if it didn't hurt. He chose to hide his wounds.

Now Israel loved Joseph more than all his children, because he was the son of his old age: and he made him a coat of many colors.
Genesis 37:3

Herman has his own way of dealing with his wounds; he doesn't. Herman is the apple of his father's eye. There is no denying this fact. Even after he became an adult, Robert continued to refer to him as "my boy." He will give Herman anything that he has in his possession. Robert is extremely proud of his son. They share a very close relationship.

Herman was not raised to hate his father. He has always been present in his life. He has never disciplined him, to do so would bring about my wrath. As a child,

Herman was also extremely close to his stepfather, Buck. Buck has never said anything negative about Robert to Herman.

Over the years, Herman had heard many negative things about his father. He didn't hear them from me. Even after reading *A Journey to Hell and Back*, he has never discussed any negative emotions concerning Robert. These emotions or feelings would have consumed him. He did not allow the seeds of bitterness and resentment to take root. He found oil for his wounds in the Word of God.

How much better to get wisdom than gold, to get insight rather than silver!

Proverbs 16:16 NIV

La'Toya, my granddaughter, had to come to terms with what happened. She tells it like this:

Until the first book came out, I never knew what happened. A lot was kept from me and initially the first book was, too. When I got the chance, I snuck and read it. I never knew that my grandma had been burned. At that age, I assumed that it was her skin and that everybody was different. I was around eight when the first book came out. At that age, I didn't know what skin grafts were.

All my life, he'd been my grandfather. He was so nice to us; he gave us food and

money. He lived down the street from my great grandma. We would walk down the street to visit him.

When I finally read the book, I was in shock. It was really hard to believe that he could have done anything that heinous. As long as I've known him, he's been somewhat weak. And honestly, I believed my grandma could take him. I never knew the old strong him. I was confused for a while after I found out, but then nothing changed for anyone else. When you're young, you just follow the cues of the adults in your family.

As an adult, whenever I see them interact, there is the thought in the back of my head. It's saying, 'Wow! I don't know if I could do it. They act as if nothing happened. I wonder if he even remembers.' Then, they start cracking jokes and he proposes to her.

For pressing milk produces curds, pressing the nose produces blood, and pressing anger produces strife.
Proverbs 30:33

Shortly after the accident, I decided to forgive Robert. Two detectives came to the hospital. They had been questioning Robert about what had happened. They wanted me to make a statement to enable them to press charges against him. My mind was made up; it was best for everyone if no one knew what had happened inside the apartment.

The morphine had made my mind cloudy; I don't remember what I said. They were standing near the foot of my bed. I wasn't willing to assist them with the investigation. It was too painful to repeat what had happened in the house. There would be a long time before I would be able to tell my mother what had occurred on this day, months after I was released from the hospital. Aunt Bobbie said that I told her one day while I was in the hospital, but I don't remember telling either of them. At some point, I began assuming that I had told Mama what happened.

"Come now, let us settle the matter," says the LORD. "Though your sins are like scarlet, they shall be as white as snow; though they are red as crimson, they shall be like wool.

Isaiah 1:18 NIV

If I had chosen to harbor seeds of bitterness towards Robert, it would have destroyed me and my children. Because I chose to forgive, they were able to do the same. They are not perfect children, but both of them are compassionate and loving. Both of them have the heart to help others in need.

In him we have redemption through his blood, the forgiveness of sins, in accordance with the riches of God's grace.

Ephesians 1:7 NIV

It didn't happen immediately, but God gave me the grace to move past mere forgiveness. With time, Robert and I became good friends. He respected me as his ex-wife and the mother of his children. He was a very generous person and for most of the time that I have known him, I was a recipient of his generosity. Whatever he had, he was always willing to share with me and my children.

Robert was known to call me and say, "Tell that boy to come by here. I have something for him." To him, Herman never grew up. He was always that boy or son. He was always kind to Herman. He would say, "Now son, listen to me." At the mention of Herman's name, Robert's eyes would light up and a big smile would come across his face. This was the child of his age.

When Herman's daughter, Alexandria was born, she brought Robert great joy. She was fond of him, too. One day, she saw Robert without his false teeth in his mouth. It scared her so bad. She screamed as loud as she could and cried. She was so scared; he had to walk away. The next time he saw her, he didn't have his teeth in his mouth. He tried to talk to her without her being able to see inside his mouth. Alexandria never forgets anything that she sees or hears and she certainly hadn't forgotten the image of Robert without his teeth. He began to scream again. She would watch his mouth whenever she saw him and scream if his teeth were not in place.

Robert was an amazing cook. He could cook almost anything. In the early years of our relationship, whenever, he would barbeque the neighbors would bring meat for him to cook. He would cook the meat free of charge and provide the barbeque sauce. His cooking abilities did little for his appetite. As he grew older, he often ate from a saucer. There were some days that he only wanted vegetable juice.

In early December of 2016, Robert was hospitalized briefly. After his release from the hospital, there seemed to be a drastic increase in his appetite. For Christmas, I sent him two plates of food. He said that he ate all of the food. A couple of days later, he called me.

Oh give thanks to the Lord, for he is good; for his steadfast love endures forever! Let Israel say, "His steadfast love endures forever." Let the house of Aaron say, "His steadfast love endures forever." Let those who fear the Lord say, "His steadfast love endures forever." Out of my distress I called on the Lord; the Lord answered me and set me free.

Psalm 118:1-5 ESV

Laughing he said, "I'm so hungry! Tell that boy to bring me some barbeque sandwiches."

Shocked, I immediately called Herman. Ironically, he answered the phone. This is something that he seldom does when I call him. This time, I called him, "Boy."

Excited that Robert wanted something to eat, I said, "Boy if your daddy is hungry take him something right away! He wants barbeque sandwiches."

He replied, "Yes, ma'am."

To my amazement, my super slow son immediately took Robert the sandwiches.

After he finished the sandwiches, Herman took him out to a restaurant to eat. Robert ate all of his food. Before dropping him off at home, Herman bought fried chicken. We were overjoyed that he was eating so much. We were also amazed.

A hot-tempered man stirs up strife, but he who is slow to anger quiets contention
Proverbs 15:18

On December 31, 2015, we received a call that Robert had passed. The last couple of years had been difficult for him. December was a hard month for him in several ways.

There were several things that happened in that month that could have caused seeds of bitterness to grow in his heart. Robert had always had a quick temper. Instead of becoming angry, he responded with a calmness I had never seen before.

That day, my children lost a father, friend, encourager, supporter, and much more. My granddaughters lost someone who loved them dearly. An era of my life came to an end. I will forever be grateful that any seeds of bitterness for him were plucked up long ago.

"Anger and bitterness are two noticeable signs of being focused on self and not trusting God's sovereignty in your life. When you believe that God causes all things to work together for good to those who belong to Him and love Him, you can respond to trials with joy instead of anger or bitterness." ~ John C. Boger

Ministries

Give it to God

"Be angry, and do not sin; do not let the sun go down on your wrath,

Ephesians 4:26 NKJV

Bitterness is not something we can simply ignore. It won't go away because we ignore it. Bitter people often make excuses for their bitterness. They blame others for their feelings. Some people even blame God.

Some Common Causes of Bitterness

Trust in the Lord and do good; dwell in the land and enjoy safe pasture. Take delight in the Lord, and he will give you the desires of your heart.

Psalm 37:3-4 (NIV)

1. Unfulfilled Goals or Expectations

When some people fail their real or imaginary goals, they become bitter. It may be easier for them to blame their unfulfilled dreams or expectations on others. This may seem easier than accepting that they lacked the skills, intellect, gifts, or sufficient motivation to achieve their goals and expectations.

Refrain from anger, and forsake wrath!
Fret not yourself; it tends only to evil.
Psalms 37:8

2. Unresolved Anger

Bitterness and anger are good friends.

When you find one, the other is likely to show up. Bitterness is often the result of an angry spirit. The Bible warns us to be angry, but sin not. Some people are controlled by hostility and anger. They are a timed bomb waiting to explode. Others express their anger outwardly. Still, others will attempt to conceal their inner rage and frustration. This too may be dangerous.

"Come now, let us settle the matter," says the LORD. "Though your sins are like scarlet, they shall be as white as snow; though they are red as crimson, they shall be like wool.
Isaiah 1:18 NIV

3. Unresolved Offenses

Conflicts with others that are unresolved are common causes of lasting bitterness and resentment. Disagreements often create deep offenses in our hearts. Angry and hurtful words are often exchanged. Offenses arise when we believe that an injustice has been committed against us. This can be a real or imagined offense.

For if you forgive other people when they sin against you, your heavenly Father will also forgive you. But if you do not forgive others their sins, your Father will not forgive your sins.
Matthew 6:14-15 NIV

4. Lack of Forgiveness

Unwillingness to forgive others is a major cause of bitterness. Some people take great pride in their commitment not to forgive. At the heart of unforgiveness is pride. "How dare they treat me like this?"

If we confess our sins, he is faithful and just and will forgive us our sins and purify us from *all unrighteousness.*

1 John 1:9 NIV

5. An Unregenerate Sinner

Those who have not accepted Jesus Christ as their Lord and Savior are least likely to forgive. They are more likely to harbor feelings of resentment.

And lead us not into temptation, but deliver us from the evil one.'

Matthew 6:13 NIV

6. Bitterness by Association

Sometimes a person will unknowingly assume the bitterness and offenses of someone else. Bitterness is truly like leprosy or HIV, which can be caught through our personal contact with a person contaminated by bitterness.

How can we get rid of Bitterness?

1. Deal with it immediately.
2. Sincerely repent. Godly sorrow worketh repentance.

3. Be willing to forgive. If we are going to be forgiven, we must be forgiving. 4. Be willing to reconcile offenses. As much as lies within us, we are to live peacefully with all men. This includes women too.

5. There are many people who claim to be a Christian but have only a **form of godliness.** The real gospel centers exclusively on Jesus Christ. We have to put Him first in our lives as Lord and King.

6. We have to acknowledge God's power.

7. We have to avoid fellowshipping with other people who hoard seeds of bitterness.

8. We have to make a consistent effort to avoid collecting seeds of bitterness.

Epilogue

For although they knew God, they did not honor him as God or give thanks to him, but they became futile in their thinking, and their foolish hearts were darkened.

Romans 1:21 ESV

God has given us good reason to forgive those who hurt us. Sometimes, it seems those "brighter days ahead" will never come. Earline asked me if this book would have a happy ending. It is my desire that every story has a happy ending. It is my prayer that after reading this book every reader will cast aside the seeds of bitterness. That's the happy ending.

Not every story has a fairy-tale ending. Sometimes, there is no forgiveness or reconciliation. There are times when the mistreatment continues unabated.

If we truly believe in the sovereignty of Almighty God, we have every reason to forgive those who hurt us. We have to rid ourselves of the seeds of bitterness.

Some say, "Forgive and forget." Others say, "I forgive you, but I will never forget." It may not be possible to forget what happened. However, the memories shouldn't cause extreme pain. I don't say that we should forget what they did to us. We will have our memories with us forever, but we can forgive even when we can't forget. To forgive means to choose not to remember the pain of the offense.

When the governor of Georgia gave me a pardon for my crimes, it meant that the state was forgiving me for my crimes as if they never happened. To pardon means to clear the record. In the world, this is not true and there are still penalties to pay. When God pardons, He throws the offense/sin into the sea of forgetfulness. When we pardon someone, it means we are giving up the right to hold on to the pain of bitterness.

This is only possible when we come to see our problems through the eyes of the Lord. When we recall the words of Jesus as he hung on the cross, it makes it possible for us to remove every seed of bitterness.

Other Titles
By
Dr. Charlotte Russell Johnson

ISBN 0974189308

ISBN 0974189316

ISBN 0974189324

ISBN 0974189332

ISBN 0974179340

ISBN 0974189359

ISBN 0974189369

ISBN 0974189375

ISBN 0974189383

Reaching Beyond, Inc.
www.charlotterjohnson.com

Helping hurting humanity to reach beyond the barriers in their life, one barrier at a time.

ORDER FORM

Know someone else in crisis or in need of encouragement order additional copies of this book to sow seeds of healing grace.

Postal Orders:

Reaching Beyond, Inc.
P. O. Box 12364
Columbus, GA 31917-2364
(706) 573-5942
Email us at: admin@charlotterjohnson.com

Please send the following book(s).

Qty.	Title	
______	*A Journey to Hell and Back*	$14.95 each
______	*The Flip Side*	$15.95 each
______	*Daddy's Hugs*	$12.95 each
______	*Grace Under Fire*	$14.95 each
______	*Mama May I*	$14.95 each
______	*Mama's Pearls*	$14.95 each
______	*Breaking the Curse*	$14.95 each
______	*Kissin' Hell Goodbye*	$14.95 each
______	*Oil for the Wounded*	$14.95 each

Sales tax:
Please add 7% for books shipped to GA addresses.
Shipment:
Book rate $3.50 for the first book and $1.75 for each additional book.

Also available at www.charlotterjohnson.com